LET'S GO AND DO LIKEWISE

LET'S GO AND DO LIKEWISE

(in loving our neighbors)

JOHN WOODRUFF

Xulon Press

Xulon Press
2301 Lucien Way #415
Maitland, FL 32751
407.339.4217
www.xulonpress.com

Unless otherwise indicated, Scripture quotations taken from the Holy
Bible, New International Version (NIV). Copyright © 1973, 1978, 1984,
2011 by Biblica, Inc.™. Used by permission. All rights reserved.

Printed in the United States of America.

ISBN-13: 978-1-6628-0896-8

ACKNOWLEDGMENTS

Special appreciation is expressed to:

My grandchildren who encouraged me to record life experiences relating to neighbor relations,

Secretary Sara Cates for word processing,

My wife, Ina, for text review, and for giving insight on what and how to record neighbor relations,

Special thanks to my friend, Gersaid Romero, used of God to make me aware of a critical medical need that I had, and for giving me motivation for writing this book,

Many Christian friends being wonderful Good Samaritan models to me and others, and

All neighbors recorded in this book, providing examples for what we should do or not do to be good neighbors.

TABLE OF CONTENTS

INTRODUCTION

In many ways, neighbor relations at personal, community, national, and international levels, are not good. Jesus gives us the command to, "Love your neighbor as yourself," to care for your neighbors, to give of self to help the neighbor in need, to treat neighbors with respect, and not to discriminate or look down on neighbors. When examining our lives, community, nation, and world, it's easy to see that neighbor relations quite often fall short of the Great Commandment's instructions for relating to neighbors. There are many good, ongoing efforts to improve neighbor relations, but most of us need to do more in reaching out to neighbors to fulfill Jesus' commandment to "Go and do likewise." This writing challenges you and me to prayerfully examine our relationships with neighbors: who they are, how we are relating to them, and what we need to do to be the Good Samaritan neighbor that we are commanded to be.

My career involved writing a lot of agricultural publications, including booklets, brochures, newsletters, and business letters to the agricultural community for improving crop productivity and profits. It involved knowledge gained from research, scientific studies, experience, and interaction with colleagues. The writing here is not based on my expertise but is written from my heart as led by Bible scriptures and the Holy Spirit. An "out of this world experience" prompted me to begin this writing. You may not agree with everything written here, but you will probably agree that our neighbors and the world could really benefit from improved neighbor relations. As you read, I challenge you to search your heart about how you can be the *good neighbor* that you are commanded to be.

I.

BLESSINGS OF A GOOD NEIGHBOR

Yours truly is alive and well at the time of this writing because of God's grace and mercy extended to me through a dear friend, Gersaid Romero. I came to know Gersaid in 2016 when we both got involved in Bible study and shared with inmates at the Tift County Jail in Tifton, Georgia. Inmates there are housed in nine-cell blocks, with about forty men per block. About half the inmates participated in Bible study and sharing each week.

We started each session with an open invitation to participate. My sharing always began with Jeremiah 29:11 (God has a plan for you). I then stated, "God's plan for your life is not for you to be here, but that He may have you here to seek Him, and to get direction for walking in the light." Each session emphasized the need to seek His leading through studying His Word, and seeking support groups, such as Celebrate Recovery, once released.

In the process of sharing, Gersaid and I became good friends. We shared life experiences and how we came to know, love, and serve Jesus. Our families also became friends. We visited each other, shared meals, and Gersaid's children occasionally came to my pond to fish. We were grateful to God for giving us the opportunity to share the Good News with the inmates, and also for the opportunities to know, love, and spend time with each other's families.

When visiting with the inmates, we centered our sharing on loving God and loving people. Scripture central to this sharing was the Great Commandment and the Good Samaritan parable. Inmates were recognized as neighbors and were encouraged to show compassion, care, love, and respect for one another. We made Bibles and daily devotionals available for them and encouraged them to receive those materials and use them daily.

THE MARCH 6 PHONE CALL

Wednesday nights usually found my wife, Ina, and myself attending a fellowship dinner and Prayer Meeting at Tifton First Baptist Church. What happened on the night of March 6, 2019 and in following days was out of this world. The experience cannot be explained by science or coincidence. I most always silence my cell phone when in church, but purposely felt led not to do so that night. After prayer time, a lady spoke to the attendees about the life, needs, and activities of missionary families in Europe and Africa who are supported by our church. As she closed in prayer, my cell phone began ringing. Startled and embarrassed, I immediately silenced it, noting that the call was from my jail ministry partner, Gersaid. I stepped outside after the prayer meeting and returned his call and assumed that it had something to do with our ministry at the jail the next night.

We greeted each other, and Gersaid asked, "How are you feeling?"

My response was, "I feel fine. Why do you ask?"

Gersaid stuttered for two or three seconds and said, "John, God told me to get out bed at 2:00 this morning and pray for you. While praying, He told me that you have a serious problem in your head." Gersaid then stated, "I have never made a phone call like this in my life, but I was given instructions to call you, to arrange to come lay hands on you, and pray for your well-being. Where can we meet?"

Needless to say, I was somewhat stunned by his statement and request. I regarded Gersaid as a devout Christian, and I could not disregard his statement and request. Gersaid asked if he could meet me that night to lay hands on me and pray for me. I had animals at home that needed attention, so I said, "Why don't we meet for prayer tomorrow night for a few minutes at the jail before going in to share with the inmates?"

Gersaid reluctantly agreed and closed, saying, "I will see you there."

I left church perplexed and wondering, *Is this real? I feel fine, there is nothing wrong with me.* I suddenly remembered a somewhat strange experience that had occurred the previous week. I had reclined in the living room after supper to watch TV. I became drowsy and almost went to sleep. After a few minutes, Ina came to the living room and asked, "What are you watching?" In attempting to say, "National Geographic," my speech went gibberish for about ten seconds before I could vocally communicate back to her. We both took note that the gibberish was strange but laughed it off as another sign of aging.

I had a routine follow-up appointment with my internist the next day, March 7, to monitor some mild blockage of the carotid artery that had been observed six months earlier. In light of Gersaid's call, Ina and I both agreed that I should mention the gibberish incident when seeing my doctor during the appointment. Before leaving for the doctor's office on March 7, I told my wife about all the activities planned for the day and asked if she could have lunch prepared early to help with my plans. I expected that the doctor's visit would take no more than an hour out of my schedule for the day.

After arriving and checking in, the nurse went through the routine checks for blood pressure, temperature, pulse, and so forth. She commented about my previous visit and the follow-up. Then she asked if there was anything else that needed to be brought to the doctor's attention. I told her about the gibberish incident, but I did not mention Gersaid's phone call the night before.

I shared the gibberish incident with my doctor. He first dismissed it as a part of not being fully awake, but said that to be on the safe side, he would schedule a CAT scan that morning. After the CAT scan, I was instructed to go back to my doctor's office for a review and assessment of the test. After waiting for several minutes in his office, he came into the room startled, saying, "The CAT scan shows you have a large mass behind your left eye; also, you have excessive brain swelling around the mass. The mass may or may not be cancerous, but you are at high risk of having a major stroke at any time, due to the swelling."

My response was, "Are you serious? I don't have any pain or symptoms." My doctor was so concerned that he would not let me walk out of the office on my own. He immediately ordered an MRI at the Tift Regional Medical Center in Tifton and asked me to call my wife to transport me to the ER. He had me wait at his office until my wife arrived; then he and his nurse escorted me to the car for transport.

Before departing, my doctor asked if it would be okay for him to call my son who is an emergency medicine doctor at Piedmont Atlanta Hospital. He wanted to tell him about the CAT scan and to pursue treatment/surgery possibilities with him. This question really got my attention, and I began to realize that I might have a more serious health issue than I previously thought.

My doctor later revealed that he had two major concerns:

1. That I had a malignant tumor, and/or
2. That I was very near to having a major stroke.

The advice he got from my son that day was:

1. To send me to Piedmont Atlanta Hospital for the MRI, as Tift Regional Medical Center is not set up to do neurosurgery.
2. It would be best if I had only one MRI with contrast at this time, and that it should be done at the place of surgery, and

3. If brain surgery was needed, Atlanta Piedmont Hospital has excellent neurosurgeons to perform the surgery.

The local ER doctor agreed to the plan and wanted to send me by way of ambulance to the hospital in Atlanta. Ina and I convinced him to let her drive me to Atlanta. At that point, I was just beginning to understand and see how God's hand, through my friend Gersaid, was preparing me for this valley that I was about to enter.

Ina and I arrived at the hospital around 6:00 p.m. Our son met us in the parking lot and escorted us to the ER desk. The paperwork for admission had been sent from my local hospital, which allowed for my immediate admission. I was assigned to Dr. David Jay McCracken, the neurosurgeon who would further assess my situation and develop a plan for further medical tests and possible surgery. He ordered an MRI and IV feeding of Vitamin K. The Vitamin K was necessary to raise my blood's clotting ability which involved lowering the blood INR to a safe level for surgery. This was crucial since I have an artificial heart valve and take coumadin blood thinner to prevent clotting. Because of a busy schedule in the lab, the MRI was scheduled for late the next day.

Dr. McCracken took the time to explain the need for immediate medical attention and that brain surgery would be likely needed. Soon after he left my room that night, my cell phone rang; the caller was Gersaid. Showing much concern, he said, "John, where are you? I came to the jail tonight, primarily to follow God's instructions for laying hands on you and praying for you."

I responded saying, "I am sorry that I didn't contact you, but medical exams today showed that I have a brain tumor. I am now hospitalized in Piedmont Atlanta and may be having surgery in the next two or three days." I apologized for not getting back to him and said, "Just pray for me now while we are connected on the phone."

Gersaid said "No! No! My instructions from God were to lay hands on you and pray for you. I will start now to make immediate plans to come to your bedside to pray."

I begged him not to come, saying, "Gersaid, you don't have to do that. You have five very young children and it's over 200 miles from your home to this hospital."

He refused to accept that response and said, "I must come. I will let you know tomorrow when I can come to see you."

That Friday, the hospital staff were busy. My MRI could not be scheduled until late afternoon. The purpose of the MRI was to get more detailed information on the type of tumor and the kind of medical treatment needed. After the MRI, I was taken back to my room and was told that Dr. McCracken would soon be calling with a report on what the MRI had revealed. My son joined Ina and me, waiting for the report. Soon thereafter, Dr. McCracken called; he described the tumor as what appeared to be a large meningioma located behind the left eye. He said the good news was that it did not appear to be a malignant tumor, but the not-so-good news was that it had caused extensive swelling of the brain, enough so that I was vulnerable to having a stroke in the near future. He went on to say that immediate surgery would be needed to remove the tumor to reduce chances of having a major stroke. My son showed a sigh of relief, as the Tifton physicians feared that the growth was a cancerous tumor. Dr. McCracken closed, saying that prepping for surgery would begin immediately and that it would likely be the next Monday, March 11, before everything could be arranged for surgery.

Reflecting on the week, I lay in bed that night awestruck at how God had brought me to this point. I had a health problem that had probably been growing/developing for years. I had come to the point where the issue could cause a stroke, take my life, or seriously reduce the quality and function of my life. How God used my friend to bring the problem to realization was just mind-boggling.

The next morning, Gersaid and his wife got a babysitter for their five children and drove over 200 miles to Atlanta and my bedside to pray for me. After a brief greeting, Gersaid placed his left hand over his left eye and said, "God tells me that you have a bad problem in your brain right here." I had not talked to him about where the CAT scan and

MRI reports had shown the tumor to be, but by this time I was firmly convinced that God had truly used this man to extend His grace and mercy to me.

As Gersaid prayed, the image of a heavily bearded man appeared before me, saying, "You will go through this valley and be okay; God is not ready to take you home. As you leave this place, you are to testify to all who will listen about your 'valley experience.' Record the experience and initiate a Heart/Hands Mission to many neighbors who have a far greater need than you have—the need for salvation to escape eternal damnation through truly knowing and trusting Jesus as Lord and Savior."

This vision was overwhelming and unlike anything I had ever experienced in my life. It was very clear. The instructions were specific: give testimony, record the experience, and be a better and truly good neighbor, filled with compassion, care, and love to help neighbors in need. The vision was so overwhelming that I did not hear what Gersaid prayed as he laid hands on me.

When he finished, he said, "God tells me that you are going to recover and be okay.

I chuckled and said, "He revealed the same thing to me, and gave me clear instructions for ministry work when I leave the hospital."

The medical staff continued prepping me for surgery that weekend. The big focus was on getting my INR down to a safe level for surgery. During that time, several friends called or came by to visit and to lift me up in prayer. I was deeply touched by the outpouring of care. Even my six-year-old granddaughter Lottie prepared a poster that said, "I Love You and Pray for You." I had a deep sense of gratitude for all the expressions of support.

On Monday, the day of the surgery, I had a great sense of peace and felt fully prepared for whatever God's loving plan might be. In the final moments before surgery, the medical staff briefed us on the surgical procedure. Dr. McCracken stated that there was a 90-plus percent chance that the surgery would go as planned, but there were risks, one of which was that I might experience a stroke or death. He stated that I would likely experience some post-surgical challenges with speech and/or vision. Then I was presented the usual informed-consent forms to sign before receiving the anesthesia. I drifted off with complete peace, feeling that God had given me assurance that the surgery would go well.

I woke up at about midnight in the ICU and remember someone telling me that the surgery was a complete success. The attending nurse came in every ten or fifteen minutes to check my physical and mental status. Each time, he would hold up several fingers and ask me, "How many?" The nurse then would move a finger up, down, and around and ask me to follow it with my eyes. After about two hours of this checking, I asked the nurse if I could share my testimony about how my need had been revealed and about how God's grace and mercy had been extended through the entire process. He said yes and became the first of hundreds of people with whom I shared about God's hand in bringing me through, and that He was preparing me for reaching out to neighbors in the days ahead.

Early the next day, I was moved back to my room to begin the recovery process. My pastor, Dr. Wayne Roe, came in to check on me and to pray for me. I was deeply touched that he had come to Atlanta to see me and could not wait to share my testimony with him.

The prepping for discharge from the hospital began that day. A main objective was to get my INR back up above 2.5. This was a slow process and would take twelve days. The medical care during this period was outstanding. There were three shifts of nursing staff each day. I gave my testimony to each of them. One day, a nurse advisor came to my room with three student nurses, coaching them on all the checks to make. Again, I shared my testimony with all of them. The nursing advisor slumped down in a chair and said, "What a friend (Gersaid) you must have! Do anything and everything you can not to lose him."

The only recovery issues that I experienced were double vision and difficulty sleeping more than an hour at a time. I had been told to expect the double vision, as the tumor had stretched the nerve going to my left eye. The sleep issue slowly resolved in about four weeks, but it took about ten weeks for the double vision to correct itself.

The extended hospital stay gave me lots of time to reflect on the vision that I had received when Gersaid had come to pray for me. He had truly followed Jesus' command of, "Go and do likewise." It was obvious that God had plans for me to go home and get involved in a Good Samaritan neighbor ministry, as He had spared me from the impending tragedy that I was about to encounter with the brain tumor.

II.

OUR COMMAND: GO AND DO LIKEWISE

As I began recovering at the hospital (and at home for the next six to eight weeks), I gave intense thought to how I should respond to the vision I had received when Gersaid came to Atlanta to pray for me. There was no doubt in my mind that God had intervened to bring my need for surgery to the attention of medical professionals, that He spoken to me in the vision, and that He had given me a charge to address neighbors in need and for penning my experience. Sharing my testimony was easy. Although sharing was highly emotional, it was a joy to get to share it with anyone or any group willing to listen. Writing is not a gift or talent for me, but per vision instructions, I gladly do it.

This health experience had left me overwhelmed for the compassion and care that had been given to me. I am not sure that I would have the guts to respond to God the way that my friend Gersaid had done for me, but I came away challenged to be more compassionate, caring, and being involved to be a good neighbor. This writing challenges you to do the same. The following chapters are presented, not as a professional, but from the heart, looking at what the Bible says about neighbor relationships. I have also shared some of my life experiences in relating to neighbors. You may not agree with everything written here, but hopefully you will be challenged to embrace the ways and actions you will need to pursue to model Christ's command to be a Good Samaritan neighbor, hereafter referred to as a good neighbor.

The big challenges for us are: how do we reach out to a neighbor in need, how do we assess and respond to needs, and how do we convey love, care, respect, and respond to the needs that our neighbors have? I invite you to also assess and respond to your neighbors' needs based on Jesus' instructions.

Seeking God's leading for being a good neighbor and discussing good neighbor relationships are not easy for me. There have been times when I have ignored the needs of neighbors and times when my attempts to reach out to neighbors have been rejected. Hence, the following chapters are written to review good and poor neighbor relationships at personal, community, and national levels and from a biblical perspective. Why should we study and assess ways to be better neighbors? Because Jesus gives us a command to do so. Improved neighbor relationships are critically needed for modeling Christ's love and for loving, respecting, and helping neighbors in need. The world will be a better place if we seek God's leading to be better neighbors.

How can we be better neighbors or good neighbors? The best place to start is to look at the biblical model for poor and good neighbor relationships:

> On one occasion, an expert in the law stood up to test Jesus. "Teacher," he asked, "what must I do to inherit eternal life?" Jesus asked, "What is written in the Law? How do you read it?" The lawyer answered, "Love the Lord your God with all your heart and with all your soul and with all your strength and all your mind and love your neighbor as yourself." "You have answered correctly," Jesus replied. "Do this and you will live." But he wanted to justify himself, so he asked Jesus, "And who is my neighbor?"

Jesus answered with a parable and said, "A man was going down the road from Jerusalem to Jericho when he fell into the hands of robbers. They stripped him of his clothes, beat him and went away, leaving him half dead. A priest happened to be going down the same road, and when he saw the man, he passed by on the other side. So too, a Levite, when he came to the place and saw him, passed on the other side of the road.

But a Samaritan, as he travelled, came to where the man was; and when he saw him, he took pity (had compassion) on him. He went to him and bandaged his wounds, pouring on oil and wine. Then he put the man on his own donkey, took him to an inn, and took care of him. The next day he took out two silver coins and gave them to the inn keeper. "Look after him," he said, and when I return, I will reimburse you for any extra expense you may have. Which of these three do you think was neighbor to the man who fell into the hands of robbers?" The lawyer replied, "The one who had mercy on him." Jesus told him "Go and do likewise." Luke 10:25-37 NIV

The compassionate, caring Samaritan of this parable is commonly referred to as The Good Samaritan or good neighbor. This scripture commandment is also presented in Matthew 22:37-40 and Mark 12:29-31. Most Bible translations refer this scripture as the great commandment. Jesus concludes the parable with the command for the young lawyer (and us) to "Go and do likewise," to be a good neighbor. The encounter of the young lawyer with Jesus speaks volumes about the kind of relationship that we should have with God and with our neighbors. The key command is love. It speaks of a vertical love relationship with God and a horizontal love relationship with our fellow man. The vertical love relationship must come first. We are created for an agape love relationship with God. We can model and return love to Him because He first loved us. We are born separated from God because of sin, but we can have that holy, righteous, loving relationship with God by the sin sacrifice given by Jesus at the cross.

This greatest sacrifice was done out of His great love that we might cross from a destiny of death to eternal life. Anyone can cross from death to life by admitting that he/she is a sinner, turning away from sin; receiving Jesus Christ as God's son by faith, accepting Jesus' gift of forgiveness from sin, and confessing faith in Jesus Christ as Savior and Lord.

The scripture cited in Luke 25:37 is commonly referred to as the Great Commandment. When asked what the scriptures say, the young lawyer was quoting Deuteronomy 6:5, "You shall love your neighbor as yourself. I am the Lord" (NIV).

WHO IS MY NEIGHBOR?

In search for ways to be a better neighbor, it would probably be good to address the question, "Who is my neighbor from worldly and biblical perspectives?" Here's what I found.

The American Heritage dictionary defines neighbor as (1) "one who lives near or next to another"; or (2) "a fellow human." These two definitions are extremes, ranging from the person(s) next door to those alive and living anywhere in the world. Another definition is "anyone that you have met or know."

From a biblical perspective, Douglas and Kimberly Wilson, in the *Holman Illustrated Bible Dictionary,* identified several biblical directives concerning treatment of a neighbor, noting that the Bible provides little definition as to what or who a neighbor is. "In Exodus 3:22 and 12:36, the term is first used in a way that crosses ethnic or national boundaries when the Israelites are instructed to borrow gold and silver jewelry from their Egyptian neighbors."

After this reference, much of the Old Testament texts concerning neighbors are either positive commands, such as Exodus 12:4 that says, "Share with your closest neighbor regarding the Passover Meal," and Leviticus 19:18, "Love your neighbor as yourself," or negative commands, such as Exodus 20:16–17, "You shall not give false testimony against your neighbor. You shall not covet your neighbor's house, his wife, his servants, his animals, or anything that belongs to your neighbor," and Leviticus 19:13, "Do not defraud or deceive your neighbor in any way" (NIV). Several scripture verses in the Book of Proverbs and the writings of the prophets also address the proper attitudes and actions one should have toward neighbors.

Caring for, respecting, helping, and loving neighbors was at the heart of Jesus' teaching in the New Testament. He emphasized these in Matthew 19:19, "Let the children come to me;" Luke 6:27-32, "Love, care for and respect, even your enemies;" Luke 11:5-8, "Friend, lend me three loaves of bread" (NIV); and especially in Luke 10:35-37 as He addressed the young attorney's question, "And who is my neighbor?"

Jesus used the parable to address, first, the command, "Love thy neighbor as thyself" and second, to address the lawyer's question, "And who is my neighbor?" From this, it appears safe to conclude that one's neighbor is not only the one next door or nearby, but anyone that you meet or observe. The contact could be direct and personal, or in today's world, it could refer to anyone in need that we are made aware of by the media or personal electronics.

After defining the loving, merciful, good neighbor, Jesus gave the command, "Go and do likewise." This command not only applied to the lawyer, but also to all mankind, both then and now, including each of us. Thus, the big question for us is: Are we willing to go and do likewise with love, compassion, and mercy, and to assume all the challenges involved?

FOUR KINDS OF NEIGHBORS

After Jesus had commended the young lawyer for correctly quoting the Great Commandment, the young lawyer, seeking to justify himself, basically asked, "Who shall I love as myself?" The Old Testament had lots of dos and don'ts about neighbor relationships, so this was a good question. Jesus' response with the Good Samaritan parable was profound. At least four kinds of neighbors are identified in the Good Samaritan parable. My pastor, Dr. Wayne Roe, in a recent sermon, defined these neighbors as follows:

1. *The Wounded Man.* The parable does not really define who he was, but he is presented as one in desperate need, and one likely to be receptive to any help from anyone, Jew or Gentile.

2. *The Thieves.* This attitude of the thieves was one that exemplified, "It's all about me." The scripture does not say how many thieves there were, but there were at least two. They were a cruel, sick kind of neighbor with the attitude, "What's yours is mine if I can take it and get away with it." They were not just thieves; they were cruel to the extent that they had stripped the man of his clothes and beat him badly. Stripping him of his clothes and beating him severely would reduce the chances of their getting caught by the authorities.

3. *The Priest and the Levite* exhibited an attitude of "What's mine is mine and is not available for sharing." This attitude was exemplified by the priest and the Levite who saw the hurt man and went to the other side of the road to avoid him. Why? The parable does not say, but they could have thought, *If I touch the man, I will be rendered unclean for performing my temple duties today.* They could have also thought, *I am too busy,* or *He is not one of us,* or *This could be a trap to catch and rob me.* Both these men made a *head* decision not to help a man in obvious need. They certainly did not model "Love my neighbor as myself."

4. *The Good Samaritan* exhibited an attitude of, "What's mine is available for helping you." The Good Samaritan was the only one who was truly a good neighbor. He saw the man in need and made a *heart* decision to help.

Note his actions. After seeing the man in need, he:

a. had compassion (an emotion of the heart),
b. came to his aid, bandaged his wounds, poured on oil and wine to treat the wounds,
c. placed him on his donkey,
d. took him to an inn for further care, rest, and recovery,
e. stayed with him overnight,
f. paid for the lodging,
g. paid the innkeeper two silver coins to take care of him, and offered to pay more the next time through, if needed.

Let us look again at the Good Samaritan neighbor model Jesus presents. The Samaritan provided bandages, oil, and wine; he placed the man on the donkey while he walked to the inn; and he paid for the lodging and care of the man. Also, and especially noteworthy, is the time he gave to help the man. For whatever reason, the Samaritan was traveling the Jericho road. He saw the man's need as urgent and more important than his plans that day. In essence, he treated the injured man the same way he would have wanted to be treated if he had been robbed and beaten.

The good neighbor model presented to us is one who cares for others, has compassion for those in need, and gives freely of himself to help a neighbor in need. On the flipside, a poor neighbor is one who tries to harm, take from, or ignore a neighbor in need. In other words, a good neighbor is willing to give of himself; the poor neighbor is all about *getting for* oneself, not *giving of* oneself.

In the Good Samaritan parable, the priest, the Levite, and the thieves made selfish head decisions; the Good Samaritan made a heart decision to help.

The mental response of neighbors getting or giving are totally different. A priest, Levite, and thief mindset must have had some level of guilt for the action or lack of action taken. Satan, at least, would love to inject guilt, having one think, *I should have ...,* or, *I could have ...!* A Good Samaritan mindset should leave one filled with the joy of the Lord, knowing that he or she has been used to help a neighbor in great need. Joy is a state of delight and well-being from knowing, honoring, and serving God. Being a good neighbor is one big way of experiencing this joy.

The Good Samaritan parable reveals that a neighbor is anyone with whom we come into contact, not just the neighbors physically living close to us. In today's world, we come into contact with people all over the world via media as well as travel. Some examples of people often with critical needs are: (1) storm victims of hurricanes and other natural disasters; (2) refugees fleeing from countries with horrible living conditions of war, poverty, violence, crime, sickness, and other atrocities; (3) homeless and poor people here in the US; (4) marginalized people; (5) children and youth; (6) incarcerated individuals; and (7) even the unborn.

WE, TOO, NEED TO BE GOOD NEIGHBORS

It's not hard to see that neighbor relations need improvement in today's world. Speaking for myself, there are people in my neighborhood that I do not know; there are very close friends and some neighbors that I find offensive for throwing trash in my driveway, discharging firearms at night, burning household garbage that generates stench, and allowing pets to run loose. I thank God for the close friends in my neighborhood. We are blessed to be able to interact, share interests such as church, gardening, and hobbies, and lift each other up in prayer, especially in times of need, but we also have the command to love the indifferent or difficult neighbor.

We Need to Get Know Neighbors, Especially Those Nearby

Many nearby neighbors do not know each other, especially in the urban world. The norm is to get acquainted with a few neighbors casually and take note of others: where they live, and maybe what vehicles they drive, and maybe speak to them in the parking lot, elevator, or in the hallway. In this setting, there seems to be more concern about security than getting to know the neighbor in the neighborhood. The world in this setting would be a better place if neighbors made more efforts to get to know each other.

A report that dominated US news in 2019 focused on a Dallas policewoman who inadvertently went up one floor too many in a high-rise apartment building to get to her apartment. She saw the front door cracked open and thought someone had broken into her apartment. She encountered a man, assumed that he was bad, drew her revolver, and shot and killed him. The man was in his own apartment, minding his own business and not bothering anyone. He was a nearby neighbor to the woman, living just above her. What a shame! What a tragedy! A mixed up, confused neighbor mistook her neighbor for an intruder, only to learn after shooting him that she was the intruder.

Nearby neighbors often get hostile with each other over petty things, such as noise, pets, boundary lines, and so on. US Senator Rand Paul from Kentucky was mowing his lawn, apparently not paying attention to the land boundary line with his neighbor. After crossing the boundary, his neighbor became hostile, stopped Senator Paul, began arguing, and then physically assaulted him. The real tragedy here is that two neighbors, living side by side, had never bothered to get to know each other well enough to care for and respect each other.

Getting to meet and know neighbors requires commitment. It takes courage for many to go over to the neighbor and introduce themselves. If they are new, the initial visit could/should be an introduction and welcome to the neighborhood. Presenting a small gift or card can be a great way to break the ice. Being a good listener is crucial to establishing a good neighbor relationship. Look for opportunities in the neighborhood where your neighbor might be walking or working outside in the yard for a brief visit. When possible, it is good to get contact information so that follow-up contacts can be made by calling, texting, or emailing.

An important first step for any planned visit is to begin with prayer asking God to prepare the way by providing wisdom, a caring and compassionate heart for the neighbor, and kind, loving, respectful words to share. Invoking God's leading and power for the visit will make a big difference in the outcome.

In my neighborhood of about 100 families, Pebblebrook Meadows, we have gone a step further in getting to know neighbors and strengthen loving and caring neighbor relationships. Five couples met in my home in July 2019 to explore ways to better get to know neighbors and to grow in compassion, care, love, and respect for one another. In our initial meeting, we decided to pursue a community activity for bringing neighbors together to introduce themselves and to tell a little about their families, careers, church, hobbies, and so forth. Ina and I have a cabin on the edge of our community, so we offered it as an initial meeting place. The core group thought it would be difficult to get the entire community together at one invitation, so each of us decided we would invite our three closest neighbors to an initial community gathering and would continue having gatherings until all 100 families had received invitations to participate.

The first gathering, September 28, went very well. About twenty couples were invited to this gathering, with the emphasis on getting to know your neighbor and sharing a little about yourself. Invitees were told there would be a potluck dinner and were asked to bring their favorite dish. In response to the invitations, fifteen families participated. It was a great time of fellowship. Everyone there said they had learned good things about their neighbors that they had not known before. I met a new neighbor I had no known, and I'm ashamed to say, one who had lived within one-third of a mile of me for over twenty years. In sharing, we learned that we had several education and hobby interests in common.

I had felt the leading of God to pursue the "Pebblebrook Get to Know Your Neighbor" initiative. I left the meeting that night feeling that it was a "Go and do likewise" event that was in line with Jesus' command for being a good neighbor.

Our group followed up with a planned Christmas party for the entire community. Initial plans were to rent a large room at the nearby Georgia Museum of Agriculture for the event. As Christmas approached, it became apparent that many of the families had church and other community conflicts and that there would not be need of a large meeting room, so we went back to arranging for the Christmas gathering to be held at the cabin. Surprisingly, about forty people were able to participate, with most bringing their favorite Christmas dish. A Pebblebrook pastor shared a Christmas message. The setting again provided a great time for fellowship and getting to know and care for nearby neighbors.

More neighborhood gatherings were planned for 2020. Unfortunately, the coronavirus pandemic stopped and interrupted these planned gatherings. Our neighborhood efforts have already created interest, cooperation, and a desire to know our neighbors better. Some of the neighbors have established a Facebook page for the neighborhood. It is being used almost daily to express concerns, needs, and interests. Yes, there were some not interested in getting to know nearby neighbors, and that is okay; we want them to know that they are welcome to participate in community activities if and when they desire.

Here are some further thoughts on ways that we can be better neighbors.

FOSTER FRIENDSHIP

Once you've met a neighbor, there are a number of things that can be done to cultivate a healthy, wholesome, caring relationship. A simple call or card might be a good start. Let them know that you were blessed to get to meet them and that you care about any needs or concerns they may have raised. You can offer to help if they express a need or concern that you might be able to help with, for example: new neighbors are usually looking for good grocery stores, doctors, dentists, service and repair shops, church families, and so on.

Recently, a new couple moved in next door. My wife and I made a point to visit and introduce ourselves. We expected to say hello, introduce ourselves, and leave, but they invited us in and began to ask a flood of questions about community services, ordinances, property lines, and fishing opportunities. The visit was great! I truly feel that a bond of friendship was established. Upon leaving, the man asked if I had any needs for which he might be able to help, adding, "Just let me know." Each day, now, when I see the man, he waves. Our thoughts now are that we should continue to make a special effort to welcome new neighbors to the neighborhood. The 2020 Covid-19 pandemic makes person-to-person contact difficult, but it should not stop us from reaching out to new neighbors. Cards, phone calls, or even across-the-fence voice contacts can be important for building good neighbor relations.

Being sensitive to neighbors' interests, concerns, and needs is an important step to cultivating a good neighbor relationship. My new neighbor is retired from law enforcement. He has some chronic health issues that limit life activities but expressed a great love for fishing. I brought to his attention that I have two ponds and extended to him an invitation to come fish at any time. He showed much interest in the invitation and says he plans to do so. Hopefully, this invitation and other interactions will strengthen our love, respect, and care for each other.

I have long struggled to be a good neighbor, not just for my neighbor next door but for all neighbors with and without obvious needs. Much of my early life, I had a priest/Levite mentality reinforced with conditional love. For forty-eight years, I was much more concerned about getting than giving. But thanks be to God, He is helping me become a more caring, compassionate neighbor.

Growing up in the '50s, I loved thumbing through the Sears and Roebuck catalog and studying products for sale. Some categories had products listed as good, better, and best. The good products were "Plain Jane" with little warranty and just enough function to get by. The *better* and *best* cost more but usually had much better warranty and reliability. God does not want us to just have a good attitude and relationships with our neighbors. He does not want us to have relationships where we simply wave or speak on occasion, but relationships that have us really seek to get to know our neighbor, his/her interests, needs, concerns, where we care about them and live in a mutual loving, caring friendship.

We need to seek *better* and *best* relationships, not only as individuals but also as communities and as a nation.

III.

LOVING NEIGHBORS AS SELF STARTS WITH A RELATIONSHIP WITH A LOVING GOD

B eing a good neighbor is all about agape love. We were created out of love for a loving relationship with God and with neighbors. Abundant life is about love. The Book of 1 John has much to say about living with a heart of love. 1 John 4:16 tells us, "God is Love, whoever lives in love, lives in God and God in them" (NIV). To live a life with compassion and love for neighbors starts with a love relationship with God. We cannot love God and hate our brother (1 John 2:11) or our neighbor. Decades ago, there was popular song, "Love and Marriage, go together like a horse and carriage." The same is true here; we cannot have true love of God without having compassion and love for our neighbor.

1 John 4:7-8 also tells us "Dear friends, let us love one another, for love comes from God. Everyone who loves has been born of God and knows God. Whoever does not love does not know God, because God is love" (NIV). In order to fully love our neighbor as ourselves, we need to grasp a bit of how much God loves us. 1 John 3:1 implies that His love is greater than our ability to comprehend. It states: "How great is the

love that the Father has lavished on us that we should be called children of God" (NIV). This means that His love is infinitely large and that as Christians, we are part of His family with eternal blessings.

We cannot just know about God's love; we must have a heart relation with Him to have and experience His love. Think again about the Great Commandment. It starts out saying, "Love the Lord God with all your *heart.*"

Scriptures say much about God's love for us:

1. It is great, beyond our comprehension (1 John 3:1)
2. God's love is perfect and unconditional, and everlasting (John 3:16)
3. Includes forgiveness of our sins (1 John 1:9)
4. Drives out fear, guilt, shame, anxiety, and doubt (4:18).

Understanding God's love helps us to love neighbors the way He loves us:

1. To be compassionate, caring for, and taking action when neighbors are in need.
2. To help neighbors, even if they are different in culture, race, religion, or social status.
3. To help neighbors, even if they are ungrateful, indifferent, or even hurtful.
4. To model and love neighbors in a way that helps them see God's love for them.

We are called to be good neighbors because God first loved us and commands us to, "Go and do likewise."

IV.

GOOD NEIGHBOR RELATIONS NEED TO START WITH PRAYER

In many cases, the most important things we can do for a neighbor in need is to pray for them. That is exactly what my friend Gersaid did for me. God revealed to him my brain tumor, a developing problem that I did not know I had. God woke Gersaid up at 2 a.m. on March 6, 2019 and told him to pray for me and to call me to tell me that I had a problem in my head. It took steps of courage for Gersaid to respond to God. Note his response:

1. He was instructed to get out of bed and pray. I cannot speak for anyone but myself, but I would have likely been confused, thinking, *Is this a crazy dream? God, are you serious? What do you want me to pray?*
2. *God, do you want me to call him with instructions to come lay hands on him and to pray for him? Will he believe me? Will he accept my request?*

What is so significant here is that Gersaid was obedient to God's instructions. I cannot say that I would have responded to God with the obedience and compassion that Gersaid did. I doubt that any other person knowing me would have responded with the same obedience that Gersaid did.

The sad truth is that many of our neighbors have critical needs, especially spiritual needs, which they do not know or understand. Many neighbors are getting trapped with substance abuse, debt, and bad relationships that are destroying them. Many, only after getting hooked, realize their need for help. We, like Gersaid, can be used in a loving, compassionate, caring way to reach out to them and help them to be overcomers. A most important thing we can do to help them is to know that God has a plan for their life that involves a love relationship with Him and neighbors. Gersaid and I, in ministering to Tift County Jail inmates, usually started by sharing with inmates Jeremiah 29:11-13: "God has a plan for your life, not to harm you, for you to have hope, and a future with Him." That you can have this relationship when you seek Him with "all your heart," that is, in seeking forgiveness of your sins, and through faith, accepting this gift of eternal life through trusting Jesus as Savior and Lord of your life and following His leading—that makes one righteous with God.

We tell the inmates that they can receive this gift by confessing their sinfulness, asking forgiveness, turning to Jesus, trusting Him as Lord and Savior, and committing to follow Him. In our local jail, about 70 percent of inmates are incarcerated for substance abuse issues. Many tell us that they are now free of the substance and do not want to get involved with it when they are released. We emphasize that it is hard to be an overcomer alone, especially if you go back to a dark environment. Most agree and ask for help. Our first step is to pray for them. First, to accept and trust Jesus as Savior and Lord, if they don't know him, and second, to be connected with a Bible-believing church and/or a support group that can counsel, encourage, and help them to be overcomers.

There's power in prayer that is beyond my ability to describe. Know that God's Word instructs us to pray. Philippians 4:6 says, "In nothing be anxious about anything, but in every situation, by prayer and petition, with thanksgiving, present your requests to God" (NIV).

Their doing so would be a great step toward helping all of us show and have the "good neighbor" traits we are commanded to have.

We need to be in persistent prayer for our youth because too many are getting trapped in substance abuse, street crimes, and suicidal tendencies. This is taking place in spite of our having one of the better education systems and career opportunities of any country in the world. Many children are growing up without adequate adult supervision, mentoring, and encouragement. Crazies with intent to harm others still have access to weapons, and children are at risk.

Children need to learn early that there is more joy in giving than getting. Poor people need more help and encouragement for getting an education and meaningful jobs. Desperate refugees especially need our love and compassion, even if they are not permitted to become citizens here. Many poor people and others need fair access to health care. This list could go on and on. All these issues need more legislative attention at the local, state, and national levels. Our political leaders need to get beyond trashing each other for political gain, giving attention to what is best for all neighbors, and pulling together to address issues for the common good of all people.

Praying for the great needs of our country is essential. This mountain can be moved if we persist. Our country needs a great revival. Please join me in praying for forgiveness where we have failed in the relationship He desires for us to have with Him and our neighbors, not just those next door, or those like us, but neighbors across our great country. Also, pray that we have boldness in the actions, love, compassion, and respect that we are called to have for each other. The Good Samaritan model does not just apply to select individuals; it applies to all neighbors. God created all mankind to be equal, of great value, and to be in loving, peaceful relationship with each other and with Him.

Gersaid and I get to share in this way with inmates at the Tift County jail each week. About 70 percent of the inmates we visit are incarcerated for substance abuse issues. Many tell us that incarceration has given them freedom from the problem, and do not want to get back into this struggle when released. We make a point to tell them, "You can't be an overcomer alone, especially if you go back into the dark environment you came from." Most agree and are willing to seek help. Our sharing with them is not professional, but just a good-neighbor effort to share our testimony, God's faithfulness, and His great love for them, as well as His desire to have a holy, righteous, loving relationship with them. Prayer is an intimate part of sharing. Most inmates openly want prayer for themselves and their families.

Recently at the jail, we shared the good news of trusting Jesus as Lord and Savior with Gerald, an inmate charged with sex trafficking. Gerald tearfully acknowledged his need to turn from a sinful life and prayed to receive Jesus as Lord and Savior. The next week, I had a request for a one-on-one visit with Gerald. I went to the visitation room, not knowing the reason for his request. When brought to me, Gerald began telling me that he had called his mother the night he had made a profession of faith and truly coming to know Jesus.

He then said that his mother began weeping and praising God. She told Gerald that she had prayed for him daily for a long time, not for his release from jail, but that God would use his incarceration to help him turn from sin and point him to a relationship with Jesus. Gerald remorsefully stated that he did not know until he called his mother that night how much she cared about his relationship with God. Gerald wanted me to know how much our sharing had blessed him and he simply wanted to say thank you. Prayer can and does make a difference. Gerald's mother did not give up; she kept praying and was overwhelmed and blessed to see how God had heard and answered her prayers.

Persistent prayer has been honored and blessed by God throughout the Bible. Hannah, the second wife of Elkanah, had been judged according to her inability to bear male children. Early in marriage,

Elkanah's other wife bore children, but Hannah did not conceive. Not only did this depress Hannah, but the other wife mocked and trashed her because she did not have children. Though hurt, Hannah persistently prayed to God for a son, and promised God, that if given a son, she would dedicate the son to Him (1 Sam. 1:11). At the perfect time, God answered Hannah's prayers, and she in turn, dedicated Samuel to God.

When God shows us a neighbor in need, He wants us to intercede in prayer. In 1 Timothy 2:1-4, Paul states, "I urge, then, first of all, that petitions, prayers, intercession and thanksgiving be made for all people—for kings and all those in authority, that we may live peaceful and quiet lives in all godliness and holiness. This is good and pleases God our Savior who wants all people to be saved and to come to a knowledge of the truth."

In many situations, intercessory prayer may be all we can do. Intercessory prayer should be the first step in getting prepared to help the neighbor in need. This was the way God involved Gersaid to inform me of my brain tumor. Without God's instruction to Gersaid and his boldness to follow, I would likely have had a major stroke.

When God speaks to us about helping a neighbor when the need is not obvious, we need to go to Him in prayer. That is what Gersaid did for me. Prayer should be an integral part of seeking to be a good neighbor. We need to seek the Holy Spirit's leading as to what to say and do when we become sensitive to a neighbor in need. Our help will be most effective if we let God lead us. With God's leading, our help may involve encouraging with a card, phone call, physical assistance, or getting the neighbor to professionals who can address their need. Whatever we do, it should be done with compassion, love, and care.

Our national leaders and others in authority constantly struggle to make good decisions and actions for peace and prosperity. They desperately need our prayers. There is an ongoing struggle between conservative and liberal leaders as to what is best for constituents. Our media is also divided, either taking sides with the left or right. As Christians, we need to be asking God to show all leaders and authorities what He desires for our country and to give political leaders and authorities wisdom and courage to lead in ways that draw all of us closer to each other and to Him. There is a desperate need for our leaders to work together in unity and to model good neighbor traits of love, care, compassion, and respect. They and our country desperately need our prayers. Pray for them daily.

V.

KNOW THAT SATAN DOESN'T WANT GOOD NEIGHBOR RELATIONS

S eeking to be a good neighbor will draw resistance and challenges from Satan. He has no interest in you or me being a good neighbor. He wants just the opposite: indifference, discrimination, broken relationships, and hate among neighbors. He loves a Hatfield versus McCoy neighbor relationship. As you take steps to be a good neighbor, expect opposition from Satan. Paul writes in 1 Peter 5:8, "Be alert and of sober mind. Your enemy the devil prowls around like a roaring lion looking for someone to devour. Resist him, standing firm in the faith" (NIV).

Satan would love to blind our sensitivity to our neighbors' needs and rob us of the joys received for helping our neighbors in need. He is constantly looking for ways to get us to a priest/Levite mindset and missing Jesus' command to, "Go and do likewise." Jesus also reminds us in John 10:10, "The thief comes only to steal and kill and destroy; I have come that they may have life, and have it to the full" (NIV).

Let us look again at the Good Samaritan story. Satan turned the eyes and hearts of at least two men to evil, not only to rob a man, but also to beat him and leave him for dead. They exhibited a sinful mentality of,

What is yours is mine if I can take it from you. Perhaps to protect themselves from getting caught and punished, they beat the man and left him for dead, knowing that a dead victim could not testify against them.

Jesus also used the Good Samaritan parable to point out that the indifferent, selfish, sinful attitude and actions of the priest and the Levite also miss the mark of being a good neighbor. Such behavior is wrong and would be encouraged by Satan, not God. Satan does not want good neighbor relations. Most people today will not try to rob and beat a neighbor, but just like the priest and Levite, some will see a person in critical need and turn away without compassion. Satan would love to have us think things like: "It's not my problem, too bad. I'm too busy," or, "He or she is not one of us." Satan would also like to have us think: "Bad things happen to bad people." I had a work associate in the 1980s when AIDS began spreading, who said, "God is punishing those sinful people; they are getting what they deserve for committing sinful acts." He could not then justify how bad things also happen to so-called 'good people.'

Satan may not cause bad things, but he uses that mentality to help block us from being good neighbors. All of us, in time, will be neighbors in need. When we, too, are in need, Satan quickly helps us feel hurt when we see indifferent or uncaring neighbors who do not offer help for our need. Satan must be applauding some of the poor neighbor relations taking place in society today. Some classic examples include businesses that run up market prices to take advantage of short supplies for storm victims, looters who steal from damaged homes, businesses that charge outrageous prices for critically-needed supplies, and recently, very high prices for medical supplies to combat the coronavirus, and also, people aware of major storms and natural disasters that destroy property, leaving neighbors without power or homeless, who choose to ignore the situation, and partisan political leaders who are more concerned about power and scoring political points than helping constituents with critical, basic needs.

WE AS A COUNTRY SHOULD BE A BETTER NEIGHBOR

Republicans and Democrats are so far split, right and left, that they do not seem to agree on the time of day, or to work together on issues that US citizens are literally begging for them to address. From Isaiah 1:18, the Lord says, "Come now, and let us reason together" (NKJV). Our leaders need to stop blaming each other for every problem and start assessing what is best for the common good of society, and reason together ways to best solve or resolve problems and issues.

I do not know about you, but it bothers me deeply to see the way US leaders manage neighbor relations with many countries. We are in verbal conflict with Mexico and Central America over handling of transit refugees fleeing to the US. Regarding Central American refugees fleeing to the US through Mexico, some Democrats say let more in and meet all their needs. Many Republicans say block their path through Mexico, build a wall, arrest and deport those who come to the US illegally. From a good neighbor perspective, there is right and wrong with both arguments. People—families—fleeing from horrific conditions need good neighbor compassion, help, and empowerment. Most of us agree that they need help, but how should we help them?

Do we simply open the border and provide for all their needs at US's expense? If one accepts this argument, and many do, then where do we stop at having good neighbor compassion for people fleeing unbearable conditions in other countries? There are more than seven billion people in the world. About one-fifth of all people live in deplorable conditions. Many of these people are desperate to flee their situation. Many in Central and South America are willing to give up everything to get to the US, hoping to find a better life. How should we respond to their desperate need while protecting the economic and well-being needs of US citizens?

To be good neighbors, do we let all migrants from Central and South America and other countries come in without appropriate documents?

This, to me, is one of the greatest good neighbor challenges facing our country. If we build all the walls possible, we fail the biblical command of, "Go and do likewise." On the other hand, allowing all people in need to come to the U S unchecked would likely overwhelm our economic, social, healthcare, and judicial systems. The real issue is, should we be compassionate good neighbors to refugees trying to escape a living hell? And if so, then how? Should we control, limit, and monitor the entry of people wanting to migrate to the US? To me, the answer is that we can't ignore it. We must work together to help both those seeking asylum and US economic and security needs.

Thankfully, many options are being explored. One possibility that should be further explored is for the Peace Corps to go into countries like Honduras and El Salvador and work there with local governments, NGOs, companies, and citizens to help supply needs and empower people on-site. Success there could reduce the incentive or urgency of families to flee. Much along this line is being done around the world, but more onsite efforts need to be pursued. The Peace Corps programs initiated by President John F. Kennedy and many others have been helpful on-site good neighbor programs. Can we build on this and other on-site programs? If so, how?

Some would argue that we can do it, but corrupt leaders would steal many of the resources supplied. Nevertheless, we should not turn and walk away. At the end of the day, on-site investments for needy people may or may not cost less than building border walls, but we cannot be good neighbors and not have compassion and help in some ways for those seeking escape from a living hell. One question is, "How do we work with or get around inept and corrupt leaders to get on-site help to people?" Supplying food, health care, and other needs can help. Working with the community and government leaders, rather than around them, can be essential for empowering them to use their God-given resources in ways to provide employment for their people and products that can meet the needs of their people or be exported.

Some developing countries have oil and minerals that, with help, can be captured to generate income. Some have land that could be made productive when modern seeds and production technologies are shared. Most developing countries fail to meet health, food, education and job needs. Helping educate and empower them to meet these needs could give a sense of confidence and reduce the need to flee to other countries.

Our overall mission should be not to just give, but to help empower them to meet their own needs. Helping empower people in their homelands could benefit all countries involved. Satan must be rejoicing when neighbors fuss and fight over ways to help neighbors in need. We must overcome and resist Satan as we proceed to, "Go and do likewise" to truly help neighbors in need.

VI.

TRULY HELPING NEIGHBORS REQUIRES BOTH ENABLING AND EMPOWERING EFFORTS OF LOVE

S teve Corbett and Brian Fikkert authored a book, *When Helping Hurts: How to alleviate poverty without hurting the poor and yourself.* They point out that poor people often have obvious and immediate needs for food, clothes, shelter, health care, and so forth. These needy people frequently ask someone to help with these needs. Corbett and Fikkert emphasize that just helping them repeatedly meet a need is usually just enabling them, not really helping or empowering them to get "out of the ditch" that they are stuck in. Poor people having these needs need more than a daily handout; they also need a source of income (or more income) to meet basic needs. They need a job to earn an income.

To really help empower the poor neighbor, make efforts in several ways to help them. Showing them a listing of available jobs, helping them prepare a resume, helping them prepare for a needed license, and helping them enroll in college or tech school for needed job training are a few. True help for a neighbor must involve more than just helping them with a handout or hand-me-downs and going on your way. Poor people often don't know their potential and just look for government and other programs to meet their daily needs. Helping them to see their potential and getting them to prepare to support themselves are big steps toward empowerment. Handouts and government programs are necessary to help meet immediate needs, but such help should be given in ways that motivate the poor person to take steps of faith for self-help and empowerment. I applaud the efforts government, community charities, and churches are doing, but if we are to be good neighbors, we can and should do more.

The concept of enabling versus empowerment is much like the old adage: *Give a man a fish, and you can feed him today; teach him how to fish, and he can feed himself for the rest of his life.*

In the following sections, I want to explore with you Christ-like ways that we might become more sensitive to our neighbors' needs and explore ways that we might get involved, not just to provide enablement, but to also help provide empowerment for meeting needs and overcoming challenges or difficulties that our neighbors face.

Let us go back and look at how the Good Samaritan acted. Out of compassion, he enabled the wounded man in the ditch. He treated and bandaged his wounds but saw that this would not be enough. These acts met the man's immediate need but did not fully empower or restore him. In order to provide for restoration, the Good Samaritan placed him on his donkey and took the wounded man to an inn so that he could get further treatment, rest, food, and care, empowering him to go on his way. In short, enabling is giving immediate help and assistance to one in need, whereas empowering is helping one get beyond his or her situation to where they can help themselves.

SOME OF MY STRUGGLES TO HELP EMPOWER NEIGHBORS

Andrew came to our church one Wednesday afternoon seeking food. One of our associate pastors, who keeps a food pantry, gave Andrew some canned foods, then invited him to Wednesday night church supper. I met Andrew there, introduced myself, and spent time visiting with him. Andrew told me that he had been displaced from the Orlando, Florida area because a hurricane had destroyed the house he was renting. He went on to say that he really liked Tifton, and that if he could find rental property, he planned to relocate here. Since I taught an adult men's Sunday School class, I invited him to join us. He did, and within two weeks, Andrew joined the church. Our church family welcomed him and was generous in helping him with basic needs.

Andrew found an inexpensive apartment on the edge of town. He had SSI income of about $750/month, and the apartment he rented cost $600/mo. This left him only $150, which was just not enough to meet basic needs each month. Andrew also had heart health issues and was in constant need of treatments and medications. He stated that he did not have sufficient health for most jobs and that he did not want to pursue employment until his health situation improved. However, Andrew was able to walk to town almost every day (about two miles) to panhandle for money. Almost every month, Andrew would go to a local hospital emergency room, seeking treatment for extreme hunger and/or chest pain. Over a period of six months, he went to four different hospital ERs with the same story. Each trip usually involved admission, tests, and heart monitoring for three to four days. It is noteworthy that all these emergency room visits occurred around the last week each month. Was Andrew using the health care system to bridge month-to-month needs? It appeared that way.

One Sunday, Andrew did not attend Sunday school or church. I called that afternoon to check on him. He stated that he had no good dress trousers for church or Sunday school attendance. He asked if some of our Sunday school benevolence fund could be provided to purchase a pair of trousers. I honored his request, picked him up at his apartment, and took him to our local mall to purchase trousers. At the mall, there were Belk's and Bealls Outlet Stores, side-by-side. I suggested the Bealls Outlet store might be best in terms of getting the most for the money.

Andrew scoffed, saying Belk's had the best-quality clothes. I overrode his request, and we went to Bealls Outlet. Andrew did find a nice pair of navy blue trousers in his size. He tried them on, and they appeared to be a near-perfect fit. In checking out, I gave the trousers to Andrew and took the receipt to have for the record showing our Sunday school class how and where the money was spent. Andrew asked for the receipt, even after I explained my reason for keeping it. He then asked the clerk if she could print him a receipt saying that it would be good to have one in case they did not fit. The clerk was a bit puzzled. I quickly stated that I would have the copy if such a need arose. I did not see Andrew wear the trousers for several Sundays. I pray that my judgment is wrong, but it appeared that Andrew was trying to use Sunday school class support money for something other than needed trousers.

A few weeks later, my wife and I were attending an Atlanta Braves baseball game three hours from home. My cell phone rang from Andrew's number, and I answered. Andrew immediately began shouting with slurred speech saying that he was in immediate need of money for food and trousers and needed a ride to Wal-Mart. My response was, "Andrew, I am not where I can help you right now." He restated the request even louder. Again, I said, "I am not where I can help you right now."

Andrew immediately responded, "I can tell you one thing, you and the First Baptist Church associate pastor are going to hell for not being willing to help the poor." After returning to Tifton, I shared the phone call with our associate pastor. He told me that Andrew had come to him for money that day and that he was obviously drunk. Neither of us ever saw Andrew again. In recent times, I have often wondered whether there was anything I could have done differently or better to help empower Andrew rather than enabling his behavior. I had wanted to help him, but failed in helping him have vision, hope, and determination for empowerment.

Looking back, I see that it was good to befriend him that first Wednesday night, and to invite him to Sunday school and church. He had testified to having a strong loving relationship with God through

Jesus. His vision statement was to get some help so that he could one day get back on his feet and work some to earn money to support himself. That seemed reasonable. All his statements seemed to be on target for empowerment, but his actions seemed totally focused on ways to get someone to give him something.

To my knowledge, Andrew never went to the Georgia Department of Labor to make application for work. Over the six months he was here, it became obvious that he was dependent on neighbors for all needs not covered in his SSI check. It was also painful to learn that Andrew was an alcoholic and was leaning on church and community to support his habit. My guess is that our church and community were not the first to support Andrew this way and that some other church community probably is doing the same now if he is still alive. Andrew, while lacking basic needs, was also a scam artist. He used a panhandler approach to get benevolence support from local churches and local charities. He did use some of the things, but likely sold some items to generate cash for alcohol. My goal was to help empower Andrew, but that could not happen without Andrew being honest and truly seeking to help himself.

Steve was another case where neighbor empowerment was a challenge, but somewhat successful. Steve started attending FBC and Sunday School about three years ago. He moved to Tifton from Fort Lauderdale and lived in a federal housing project and received just enough SSI to barely get by. He had a major challenge also being an alcoholic. He came to FBC seeking benevolence help and was receptive to getting help for his problem with alcohol. Through counseling, our associate pastor led Steve to a saving relationship with our Lord Jesus Christ. He started participating in Celebrate Recovery, a wonderful Christ-centered program for helping people with destructive habits, hurts, and hang-ups.

Steve was receptive to the empowerment progress. He went a full year without alcohol, got married, joined FBC, and regularly participated in church activities. In Sunday school, Steve praised God and church/community services for helping him recover. He did express a need to earn additional income but did not want a full-time job that would reduce his SSI income. Steve, now being married, also expressed a need for a reliable used car. He confessed that it was a daily struggle to be free of alcohol but rejoiced that he was an overcomer.

I began praying about how I could best help empower Steve to help himself. A possible answer seemed to come after Hurricane Michael blew through our area in the fall of 2018. The storm blew down trees, damaged houses and properties, and left lots of debris around Tifton needing clean up. I offered Steve my truck, trailer, tools, and my labor to help him if he wanted to get involved in cleanup and yard repair work. He eagerly took me up on the offer. We did one fence repair/replacement project that generated $2,500. Steve expressed some interest in becoming an Uber driver, then went shopping for a car. I reminded him that only select cars would qualify for Uber services. He did find a large used car with 90,000 miles, priced at $4,500 and asked me to help assess its potential. We test drove the car; it seemed to be okay. I suggested that he look further at a smaller car that would be cheaper to operate. The larger car also did not meet qualifications for Uber, but Steve was insistent on getting it and using the yard work income for a down payment. To my disappointment, he went ahead with the purchase. About one week later, the insurance company, using VIN information, discovered that the mileage information presented for the car was incorrect. The car Steve purchased had about 190,000 miles, not the 90,000 reported at the time of the sale. Steve was heartsick that he had been deceived. He also discovered another problem with the electronics that caused cranking problems for the car.

Steve had the car towed back to the dealer and demanded a refund; the dealer refused. Steve got legal counseling and filed a lawsuit. The case is pending and may take two or three years to resolve. The offense left Steve mentally crushed. He went on an alcoholic drinking binge and broke the promise he had made to himself and his wife that he would not drink again. Seeing his fault, Steve became very depressed. Steve had deep regrets about turning to alcohol in his time of depression, especially after going over a year without a drink. He is committed to starting over again in the battle to get free of alcohol. Steve realizes that he cannot win this battle with his own strength. He daily looks to God and his Celebrate Recovery support group for help, guidance, and encouragement for winning this battle. He continues to look for a part-time job to help with his need for extra finances.

What comes to the surface with Andrew and Steve is that most struggling people need good neighbors. Andrew sought to meet his needs by manipulating and scamming his neighbors. Steve, with similar struggles, sought help and support from his neighbors and church. He knew that he needed help to be an overcomer. His Celebrate Recovery support group, associate pastor, and church family are working to help empower him. Thankfully, Steve is receptive to the various empowering helps offered. Steve's receptiveness to receiving empowering help is encouraging to neighbors who reach out to help him.

There are many in need like Andrew and Steve, seeking help, trapped with mindsets like, "I failed; I can't do it; Nobody cares, or I don't want empowerment. Just give me something and don't judge my intentions." All of us encounter these kinds of neighbors, often with uncertainty about how to really help them.

One night at church recently, I was waiting in the car to pick up my wife from choir practice. Beth, a frail middle-aged woman approached me. She told me that she was hungry and thirsty. She then asked me to give her $20 for food. My reaction was "This woman is high on something and really seeking money for another fix." She also told me that she was from Louisville, Kentucky, homeless, and living under a bridge with no means of supporting herself. Beth was begging for help. I had compassion for her but did not believe she was being truthful.

I told her that I'd had bad experiences in the past giving people money for food or clothes, only to learn later that they were really seeking money to feed an addiction. She said "I'm hungry; I really need money for food. Yes, I did have a struggle with alcohol and cocaine, but I'm free of that, thanks be to God." I wanted to believe her, but I did not.

45

Soul searching, I began to ask questions to see if there was something I could do to help empower her other than just giving her the money she was requesting. When I asked her about her relationship with God, she said, "It's good. Jesus is my Lord, and somehow He is going to get me through this difficult time."

I asked her if she had sought lodging help for the homeless. Her answer was that an agency may be able to help her next week. I asked her if she had contacted local relief organizations that provided food and other assistance to marginalized people. She said, "Yes, but not recently." I then asked her what her work interests and experiences were, and if she was seeking employment. She said, "I have work experience as a cook and maid, but I can't get a job right now because someone stole my Social Security card and I don't know the numbers on it."

My wife came up at this time. They greeted, and then Beth abruptly left to engage someone else leaving the church building. Did I do the right thing not giving her money? My head thought was yes, but my heart said no. After leaving, I began to feel like the priest and the Levite. I lay in bed a long time that night, wondering what I could or should have done. Needless to say, I did not sleep well that night.

The question remains, "How do you really help someone like this, begging for money?" Encounters like this are commonplace today. If I should live so long, there will likely be similar encounters. With prayer, I began to plan to be a better neighbor for the next similar encounter. The next day, I went to McDonalds and purchased two $5.00 gift cards to give the next person requesting money for food. Along with that, I have prepared a card about where to find help, physical and spiritual. Being a Gideon, I have small Gideon New Testaments, and I have placed the gift cards in each New Testament and placed them in the center console of my truck and car. My prayer is that the next such encounter will reveal me as a more compassionate, trusting person, able to empower the one in need without enabling addiction.

Should the good neighbor encourage one seeking money to get employment or a better job? I think so, if he/she has the mental and physical capacity to work. Getting a desired job may require training, license permit, GED, and/or other testing. Giving the person in need encouragement, maybe financial support, and vision ("Yes, you can do it!") can help build their confidence for pursuing needed employment.

The Christian Women's Job Corps organization here in Tifton is helping women in need of employment get a job or a better job. In Tifton, many young women do not finish high school, often because of pregnancy and/or children. The need and value of a high school diploma comes to full reality as they start seeking employment. Many jobs require at least a high school diploma. The Christian Women's Job Corps here has several volunteer teachers who help women with course work and preparation for taking the GED exam. Women in need are made aware of this help/empowering program through DFACS and other agencies. About twelve to fifteen needy women go through this program in Tifton each year. Approximately half of them succeed in getting their GED, and most graduates are able to get gainful jobs. This is a beautiful example of reaching neighbors in need in a way that empowers them to help themselves. It involves commitment from neighbors on both sides, a compassionately caring person with needed educational skills, and a woman needing help with commitment to seek employment. To learn more about Christian Woman's Job Corps check out www.Loveyourneighborministries.com.

VII.

THE GOOD NEIGHBOR
SHOULD BE GENEROUS

I grew up on a farm in rural northwest Florida and was one of six children. Everyone in the family had work assignments to help generate income and to keep down hired labor costs. Our lives were often challenged to cover costs for the basics: food, clothing, medical, and shelter expenses. Generous giving was not an opportunity for my father. He did give a tithe to the church but was very frugal with all other spending. The family dwelling suffered a fire six months before I was born. The fire destroyed everything in the house, including several kitchen appliances that were bought on credit. With that setback and previous setbacks during the Great Depression, he literally clung to every penny earned. Mother sewed and made most of the clothes for us children. With the money struggle, I did not grow up with a heart for giving and sharing.

My attitude toward money, tithing, generosity, sharing, and helping others was much like my father's. His lack of generosity may be justified to some extent because of his growing up poor, supporting a family through the Great Depression, and struggling hard to purchase and operate a farming business, but my lack of generosity should not have been. My basic life needs were met without great struggle. My background has made me appreciate frugality, but God constantly challenges me to be a giving person with finances and time. In response, my wife and I have sought to tithe our income to the church, to give generously to support our children and grandchildren with college expenses and give to charities and Christian missions. We also give of our time in teaching Sunday school, mentoring students, helping with English tutoring for Chinese students, and helping poor people of Tanzania and Haiti with sustainable food production.

This writing on generosity is not about saying, "Hey, look at me," but is to remind me and you that we cannot strive to be good neighbors without having generous hearts—not only for giving back to God through the church, but also to neighbors in need (on the street, those experiencing unexpected storms, and especially young people in ways to help them empower themselves). After coming to know and trust Jesus as Savior and Lord, I began to gain security in the generosity of giving of time and resources and turn away from just getting. True joy of life became more and more real as I learned to give. In doing so, I began to learn that God is the great giver as well as a great loving God. John 3:16 speaks so clearly of His great, giving love.

Sad to say, we live in a world where, for most, life is all about getting, (like the thieves, the priest and the Levite), and not about giving (as exemplified by the Good Samaritan). The world at large does not know, understand, or follow the Great Commandment. A lot of us have grown from children, to youth, and to adults with the mindset, "It's all about me." This mentality is strongly encouraged by the world as it bathes us with, "Look after yourself. Life only goes around once; get all the gusto you can. Seek to be number one." Someone once said that this kind of life focus is, "Get all you can, can all you get, then sit on your can."

In addition to being born with a sinful, self-centered nature, many grow up becoming trapped in the sinful mindset of, "Get all you can and keep it for yourself." As Christians, though, we are called to reject the selfish, sinful world philosophies of caring only for ourselves and maybe a few close friends. We must get beyond this mentality to be a loving neighbor. Being generous is not easy, at least for me, but it is so important, challenging us to think and act contrary to the world's influence. God's Word is clear: Be generous. Rely on Him and His Word, not what the world would have us think and do. Only in loving and trusting God, can we have a Good Samaritan mindset.

Here are some further thoughts about why we should be generous in giving of our time and resources.

First, God is generous. He has given all of us, life, breath, and all things/resources that we have (Acts 17:25). He created this world with all the resources needed for human life. He has given man authority and dominion over the earth and its resources. He gives us capacity for love because He first loved us. His love for us is greater than our comprehension (1 John 1:3).

His greatest display of love and generosity is salvation, redemption from sin and self, offered to those who turn away from sin and toward knowing and trusting His Son for righteousness and eternal life. As He has given to us, we in turn, should be generous in giving to our neighbors. This applies even if they are different from us in culture, race, spiritual belief, worldview, or even if they are our enemy. Luke 6:35 says that in our giving, we should expect nothing in return: "But love your enemies, do good to them, and lend to them without expecting to get anything back. Then your reward will be great, and you will be children of the Most High, because He is kind to the ungrateful and wicked" (NIV).

Second, we can be generous because God is our sufficiency. First, Timothy 6:17 says, "Command those rich in this present world not to be arrogant, nor to put their hope in wealth, which is so uncertain, but to put their hope in God, who richly supplies us with everything for our enjoyment" (NIV). With this hope, we have no reason to cling tightly to wealth and earthly things. Instead, we are commanded "to do good, to be rich in good works, to be generous and ready to share" (1 Tim. 6:18). The apostle Paul further emphasized God's sufficiency in 2 Corinthians 9:8, stating that, "God is able to bless you abundantly, so that in all things at all times, having all that you need, you will abound in every good work" (NIV).

Third, we are blessed to be a blessing. As Christians, we are truly blessed in so many ways. The beautiful song, *Count Your Blessings, Name them One by One* reminds us that God showers us with many, many blessings, many of which are taken for granted. Hence, if we are to love our neighbor as ourselves, we are to let His love and blessings flow through us.

Fourth, God uses our generosity to help conform us into Christ's image. God is almighty. He doesn't need our time or money. He does reach out to our neighbors in countless ways, but He also gives us opportunity, and even tests us, in reaching out and being generous in helping our neighbor in need. Practicing generosity helps us to outgrow selfish love for things of the world, and frees us to, "Go and do likewise" in serving Christ. Jesus warned that, "No one can serve two masters. Either you will hate the one and love the other or you will be devoted to the one and despise the other. You cannot serve both God and money" (Luke 16:13 NIV).

Generosity in giving is a lifestyle that helps each of us get beyond a self-centered life to one that is God-focused and God-centered. Only at this level of spiritual maturity can we experience true joy and happiness to the fullest.

Finally, we not only need to practice generosity ourselves, but we also need to encourage it. This was the command that Jesus gave to the young attorney when He said, "Go and do likewise." People are watching. When one gives his seat on a bus to an elderly person, people around take notice and others are encouraged to do likewise, seeing it as the right thing to do. When a child is taught to share toys, candy, and so on, with other children, others learn to do likewise. When people see others reaching out to people in need, whether it be storm victims, the poor and hungry, or people without money to pay for medical treatment, they are encouraged to get involved.

Look again at what the good Samaritan gave. He gave of his resources (oil and wine), his time, his donkey (to give the wounded man a ride), his money (to pay for lodging and food), his time (to stay with the wounded man overnight), and commitment (to pay for any further expenses incurred). This parable exemplifies the essence of generous giving to be a good neighbor. We all can probably agree that the good neighbor should have a compassionate heart to the neighbor in need. Having compassion is much more likely for the one who is already generous in giving of their time and resources.

VIII.

REAL WEALTH COMES WITH GIVING IN LOVE

Many people invest lots of money buying lottery tickets, especially when the jackpot reaches the hundreds of millions. The dream thoughts are around getting lots of money for material things that will meet all their life needs and more. Some think, "If I can win, I can ditch this job, I can really enjoy life, I can even help family and friends enjoy the good life." Sad to say, they are encouraged to think this way by those promoting and operating lotteries. Also, sad to say, some of the people winning lotteries make such selfish poor choices in spending the jackpot that they end up broke and broken.

As strange as it may sound, real wealth comes from giving of yourself. Giving of time, resources, and caring for people in need to help empower them can bring a wealth of joy, happiness, and peace that money can't buy. Look again at the Good Samaritan story and the three kinds of neighbors. Their responses to the wounded man reinforce this.

The thief mindset of, "What's yours is mine" usually leaves one exerting great effort to hide or justify their actions. After robbing and hurting a neighbor, the thief has to be on constant guard, hoping authorities wouldn't catch and punish them. It takes a sick or childish mind to find peace, joy, and happiness in being a thief. People with this mentality are likely caught up in such self-defense and lack of trust that their relationships, even with those close to them, are guarded and poor. With this mentality, they must constantly stay on the defense, missing out on the real peace, joy, and happiness in life that can be obtained from loving neighbors as self.

The priest/Levite mentality of, "What's mine is mine" also misses out on true peace, joy, and happiness. Seeing a neighbor in need, then turning and walking away, offering no help, also presents a mentality that oneself and getting are more important than giving. One with such a priest/Levite mentality who turns away from a neighbor in obvious need must, at least to some extent, try to justify their inaction. Such justification could be, "He's not one of us; he had no business traveling alone," "I'm sorry for the man, but I'm too busy," or "Lord, you see the man in need; please send someone to help him." People with this mentality surely must experience some level of guilt, seeing a neighbor in need and choosing to do nothing to help. The priest/Levite neighbor surely cannot receive peace, joy, or happiness in trying to justify such an unloving action toward a neighbor in need.

The Good Samaritan mentality of, "What's mine is yours," not only has compassion for a neighbor in need, but also gives of one's time, assistance, and resources. Loving your neighbor this way gets one beyond self to reap the peace, joy, and happiness in knowing that you can be used of God to make a positive difference in the neighbor's life. Loving our neighbor as God commands brings a great wealth that money cannot buy.

Living and honoring the Great Commandment first requires obedience to God, to love Him with all our heart, soul, strength, and mind. In loving God, we are giving back to Him out of the great love He has for us when we reach out to help to help a neighbor in need. When we give of self by helping our neighbor, we honor God. Such does not go unnoticed by God. Listed here are some of the blessings we receive by being a good neighbor.

Great joy and blessing can be received in being a good neighbor

> We fulfill the Great Commandment and honor God
> We receive joy
> Modeling Christ points others to Christ
> When we give, neighbors learn also to give
> Peace/Care replaces discord and strife; and
> God is glorified.

IX.

LET GOD'S LOVE FLOW THROUGH YOU

S ince a good neighbor revealed my health need in March 2019, I have been obsessed with being a good neighbor, "Going and doing likewise." In addition to writing these memories, I have daily tried to be better/good neighbor in public, in church, and in my neighborhood. I have tried to reach out to and help people express needs in ways that might help empower them. Some efforts include regular sharing with and offering encouragement to inmates at the Tift County Jail, organizing and holding good neighbor gatherings at my house, befriending and visiting a needy elderly man weekly, trying to help a friend get a job, and making many personal contacts in the way of cards, calls, and visits.

Even with all my efforts to be a good neighbor, I must confess that there is still a lot of "priest and Levite" attitude in me. In some encounters, judgmental attitudes prevail in my mind, such as, "Why don't you try getting a job?" "Are you not really asking for support to get more bad substances that will destroy your body?" "Why don't you go to a church or some relief organization to get help?" "Why don't you say thank you for the help given?" "Why do you not seek a plan for empowerment?" "Why don't you seek professional help?" "Why are you blaming the government and others for your problems?"

The truth is that many people in need have made poor choices and often repeat poor choices. When they ask for money to buy food, it is easy to doubt them, to believe that they are not truthful, that they are putting up a deceptive front to get support for something that will further hurt them in the long run. A friend of mine was approached by a woman with a baby in her arms. She asked him for money, saying that she was desperate to get diapers for her baby. He was hesitant to give her money but wanted to help. There was a pharmacy across the street, so he told her, "Go with me there, and I will buy diapers for the baby. After buying the diapers and leaving the pharmacy, my friend wished the woman well and got into his vehicle. He looked back and saw the woman go back into the store. He watched in disbelief as the woman he thought he was helping returned the diapers to get a refund. He was hurt, realizing that he had been tricked and that he was probably supporting an addiction.

The homeless woman who asked me for money for a soda and "real food," was probably not truthful, either. When I explored her long-term needs for shelter, job, food, clothing, health, and her relationship with Christ, she had a quick answer for every question. If I could "just help her that night," she said, she had a plan for getting in a sheltered home for women the next Monday and would be seeking a job as soon as she could get another copy of her Social Security number that had been stolen earlier. I continue to agonize over my decision not to try to help her that night, not knowing a process to help empower her. It was startling to learn the next Tuesday that she had been raped and murdered at the Albany, Georgia, bus station. This happened at the time she assured me that she was to be admitted to a shelter for battered women. She was reported to be drunk, begging for money, then beaten, robbed (of what?), and murdered at the bus station in front of several people.

Could I, should I, have done anything the Wednesday before that would have help lead her to life, not death? The only positive that I can draw from my encounter with her was that I did not contribute to the alcohol or substance that placed her in such a vulnerable position at the bus station that following Monday. Looking back, I see that I failed in being the good neighbor that might have saved this woman.

How, then, do we as Christians make good decisions for helping neighbors in need? The decision is easy when the need is obvious. Seeing an obvious need, such as auto accident, house fire, storm damage, or sudden health stress should invite immediate response to get directly involved and/or to call 911. For less obvious needs, gaining insight and asking questions may help. Having compassion, giving of time and self should always be on the heart of being a good neighbor. My challenge to you—and to myself—is to be prepared the next time a sudden neighbor need arises. Include in the prayer for each day: "God, help me be a good neighbor to someone today. Show me how to respond with compassion and a loving and caring response that helps empower when encountering someone asking for help."

Keep a list with you of local churches, relief organizations, charities, and so forth that might be available for help when you simply cannot provide the assistance sought. My friend's suggestion of keeping a fast food restaurant gift card in your vehicle is a good one. When someone asks for money to buy food and you have doubts about their truthfulness, giving such a gift card will ensure that the need they ask for will be met. Including with the gift a scripture and list of local charities and relief help organizations may also be a step toward helping empower them. Good neighbor relations start with following God's commandment to have compassion when confronted with a need. It also must involve making a commitment to getting others, including community and government leaders, involved for ongoing neighbor needs, and especially for special needs people and the poor.

Let us take another look at some of the neighbor needs facing our community, state, and nation, especially needs for our youth and the poor. Many youths are struggling with peer pressure, substance abuse, sex, and street violence. They lack vision and hope for their-God given potential. We do have many great community efforts to help empower children to help themselves and to help them become responsible

61

citizens, but too many are getting involved in substance abuse and turning to gangs and criminal activity. Are there additional things parents, churches, and communities can do to empower children? Can we give more to support charity organizations? Can we foster a child from a dysfunctional home situation? Can we mentor a child within our family, church, or community in ways to help them become responsible, respectful, contributing adults? Pray about it. Let God show you ways to give empowering help to young people in need.

Drugs are a major problem, literally demoralizing and destroying many, especially youth. It's time to seriously declare war on bad drugs coming into the US, and those produced here. We need to start making the young child fully aware of the enticement and trap that drugs create. They need to know about the trap they are facing and be aware of the one tempting and trying to destroy them. There needs to be wholesome activities for the child from waking moments in morning until bedtime. The statement, "An idle mind is the devil's workshop" is so true. Caring, loving parents must see that their children stay mentally and physically active much of each day. Physical exercise is good, not only for helping create a healthy body, but also for helping learn rules, regulations, and respect for others.

Helping children learn a good work ethic at a young age can be an important step to helping them be responsible adults. Do not hold back! Parents, require and help your children learn to work and assume responsibilities. Assigning them chores like making up their bed, taking out trash, feeding the pet, picking up and storing toys are some responsibilities to start with. While chores are good, never assign any that might endanger their health. Give your children an allowance for assigned work. Daily, find ways to encourage them and ways to build their self-confidence. When needed, discipline them in love.

Spend time with them. Read stories to them before bedtime. Play games with them. Take them to Sunday school and church. Share your faith with them. Let them hear and know your testimony. Let them know that they are created by God, that He created them uniquely to be who they are.

Find ways to reach out to children in your church, school, and community charities. Just about every organization offering programs for youth can use volunteers to help with activities. If you can't get directly involved, check to see if there are ways to provide financial support.

Study the special gifts and talents of children around you. Help them have vision to see their potential in these areas. Encourage them to think and to dream of being the best at that gift one day. If their talent is music or sports or art, give them historical examples of people who, when young, were encouraged by someone, and how their dream was realized. Invest in musical instruments, sports equipment, art supplies, or whatever so that the child can exercise his or her gift or talent. If needed, invest in instructors to help them develop their talents. Explore the many programs currently available; Boys and Girls clubs, Boy Scouts, Girl Scouts, 4-H Clubs, Young Life, and numerous others offer much for helping children prepare for wholesome adult life. My own life is a testimony to the encouragement, guidance, and confidence gained through the 4-H club. For a list of youth organizations that you might contribute to or get directly involved, see www. Loveyourneighborministries.com.

WHY WE MUST HAVE A LOVE RELATIONSHIP WITH GOD FIRST

> The second part of the Great Commandment of "Love Your Neighbor as Yourself" cannot be carried out until we honor the first part. "Love the Lord your God with all your heart and with all your soul and with all your strength and with all your mind."

WHY?

1. His love is unconditional
2. His love is greater than our comprehension
3. His love is sacrificial, all about giving
4. His love has no boundaries; it even includes enemies; and
5. His love is everlasting/eternal (for believers).

FOR BELIEVERS, THIS LOVE FLOWING THROUGH US SHOULD BE (FROM 1 CORINTHIANS 13:1-7)

1. Long-suffering
2. Kind
3. Not envious
4. Not promoting itself
5. Not behaving in an unbecoming fashion
6. Not seeking its own things
7. Not easily provoked
8. Believing the best about people, not keeping a record of wrongs, or "thinks no evil"
9. Not finding joy in unrighteousness but rejoicing in the truth
10. Always protecting, trusting, hoping, and persevering.

X.

SOME CHRIST-LIKE MODELS FOR LOVING NEIGHBORS

We are blessed to have many individuals and organizations who are giving of themselves to help neighbors in need. Three that I especially appreciate are listed here. One beautiful effort for the on-site empowerment of people took place in Rwanda. During the 1990s, there was war between the Hutu and Tutsi tribes in Rwanda. The war was intense, with the killing of many men in both tribes. Women and children from these families were left extremely stressed and were facing starvation. Most had income of less than one dollar a day, but the women did have expertise with basket weaving. An American businesswoman, Willa Shalit, saw their extreme struggle and observed their basket-weaving talent. She envisioned that there would great marketing opportunities if the products were exposed to world markets, so she helped to establish the Path to Peace collection of crafts for Macy's and other markets. A picture of two of these very beautiful handbaskets is shown below.

This exquisite work of art was handwoven by the famed Gahaya master weavers exclusively for the Path to Peace collection. It was inspired by a traditional Rwandan design and handwoven, using centuries-old techniques. Sales of these baskets at Macy's department stores and online allowed many Rwandan women to move from extreme poverty to having adequate income to feed and educate their children, gain access to health care, and assume leadership in the community. This good-neighbor effort is a great success story for helping empower Rwandan women in ways that allowed them to help themselves.

Another person with a true good neighbor heart is Graham Huff from Atlanta. He, through League of Hope ministries, is working with

Haitians to help empower them. One great need in Haiti is for getting more protein into the diets of children. In one project, Graham has coordinated ministries of the South Carolina Episcopal church with the University of Georgia, Fort Valley State University, and the Georgia peanut industry to improve and increase production of peanuts and to process them into a peanut-milk food for children. The efforts are also providing a new market for Haitian farmers. In the same mission, Graham has coordinated efforts to increase and improve goat meat and milk production. His heart for helping Haitians and skills for coordinating participants are starting to show promise.

The Carter family of Plains, Georgia, are great good-neighbor models for the world today. As a young woman, President Jimmy Carter's mother Lillian trained to be a nurse. Finding herself a mother of four young children in Plains, she provided medical care and assistance to poor people who could not afford such care. In her sixties, she joined the Peace Corps and spent two years in India helping very poor people, mostly lepers, with medical needs. President Carter and his wife Rosalynn followed in the footsteps of his mother's good-neighbor heart. After his presidency, Jimmy and Rosalynn have devoted much of their lives to helping people in need. They worked with Habitat for Humanity to provide quality affordable housing for poor families. They have worked with leaders in African countries to combat and help eradicate infectious diseases. They are true good-neighbor models for helping empower needy people. Their work is ongoing through The Carter Center that is devoted to human rights and the alleviation of human suffering. What joy they must have in going and doing likewise. To learn more about their ministry or to make a financial contribution to their ministry, go to cartercenter.org.

These are just three of many wonderful on-site efforts to help people. Helping empower people on-site requires working with local governments, churches, and other organizations to identify needs and develop a focused plan for meeting needs where all parties can team up and work together to address them. Most good neighbor efforts involve a team effort, people seeing a need, praying for God's leading, soliciting support and volunteers, and taking action to carry out the plan. Regular meetings of all participants are essential to assess progress and to hold all parties involved accountable.

One could argue, "Wow, such effort will cost lots of money and even more time." Yes, but building walls, border security operations, deportation expenses, and other efforts also cost lots of money and effort. But giving and helping in whatever way honors the command of, "Go and do likewise." We should not look the other way and ignore the Central American or any other human crisis. Like the Good Samaritan, we need to go on-site to bandage wounds, provide care, and help empower them.

Hurricane Dorian went through the Bahamas in 2019 destroying homes, infrastructure, and people. The damage was obvious and was reported worldwide. Thankfully, aid came from lots of people and countries. Seeing the devastation and great need of all storm victims should prompt all of us to a least contribute money and/or basic supplies to help them recover. The American Red Cross and other quality relief organizations provide help to victims of natural disasters. See www. Loveyourneighborministries.com for ways you can help any of these neighbors in need.

XI.

LET'S LOVE AND RESPECT ALL NEIGHBORS

There is a tendency for good neighbor relations to be restricted to those like ourselves. In the Good Samaritan parable, help was given by a Samaritan to the wounded man, likely one from a different culture and background. Jesus used this parable to show that good neighbor relations should apply to everyone. Sad to say, we live in a society where many people show prejudice, discrimination, and/or rejection to neighbors different from themselves, based on race, wealth, culture, or religion. Neighbors who have been looked down upon, rejected, or discriminated against rightly respond with hurt, anger, resentment, and demands for equal rights.

From a scriptural viewpoint, all people are created equal. None of us have superior status over others in creation. God loves all people, regardless of race, culture, or wealth status. Jews were a chosen, but not superior, race. At the time of Jesus, they looked down on Samaritans and Gentiles, people they generally considered unclean and unworthy of care as neighbors. Jesus rebuked this as He fully declared God's love for all people. He lived, served, and died that all might have a righteous relationship with God. Classic examples are not only the Good Samaritan Parable, but His reaching out to the centurion, to Nicodemus, to the Samaritan woman at the well, little children, and many others.

James, in writing to the twelve tribes after Jesus's crucifixion, warned against showing favoritism or giving any superior status to the rich. He said, "Have you not shown partiality among yourselves and become judges with evil thoughts" (James 2:4 NKJV). He went on to say, "Listen my brothers, has not God chosen those who are poor in the eyes of the world to be rich in faith and to inherit the kingdom he promised those who love Him?" (James 2:5-6 NIV).

The message should be clear. God has created all people of all tribes and nations out of His great love for all. He did not create any of us to be prideful or arrogant, or to discriminate against any neighbor. For us to love our neighbors as ourselves and model His love, we must not discriminate against our neighbors or look the other way when any neighbor discriminates against another. While US civil rights legislation has helped reduce discrimination, it has not changed the hearts of many with racist/discriminatory agendas. It is time that we further address the need for improved neighbor relations between races and cultures from moral and spiritual perspectives. Jesus did just this in sharing the Good Samaritan parable.

Who helped the wounded man in need? It was not the priest or the Levite, both of whom knew God's laws for neighbor relations. It was a Samaritan, a man of a different race and culture. The priest and Levite made a no-help head decision, with likely attitudes of, "He's not one of us," or, "It's not my problem." Jesus was deliberate in contrasting the self-centered head decisions of the priest and Levite with the heart-centered compassionate decision of the Samaritan who put his agenda aside to provide whatever help was needed.

What would Jesus instruct us today to be better neighbors, especially between races? Here are my thoughts about what He would say:

1. We were created by God for a love relationship with Him and our neighbors.
2. He created each of us to be unique, but equal. (He didn't create any of us to be arrogant, or to look down upon or discriminate against any person regardless of race or social status.)

3. He created each of us to love, care for, and respect our neighbors.
4. We are to look to His Word for guidance in doing so.
5. We are instructed to pray for all our neighbors.
6. We are commanded to, "Go and do likewise," helping all neighbors in need.
7. We are to take a stand against Satan and those who would mistreat, discriminate against, or ignore neighbor needs.

What is crucial to good neighbor relations is to know that we are all in this together, created by Almighty God to be in a love relationship with Him and each other. We have a command to love, care for, and respect each other regardless of race, sex, culture, religion, or country.

Yes, we are all imperfect with faults, but we need to look beyond these, seeing each other as God's creation and pursuing ways to see this, having the mindset and the heart-set of the Good Samaritan. Alone, we cannot do a lot to accomplish this. But we most likely can fulfill the command of, "Go and do likewise" if we organize a movement to bring this need to the attention of the populace and encourage good neighbor relations.

The lack of good neighbor relations among races, ethnic groups, religions, and immigrants is a growing social issue for our country. We have laws and mandates for equal rights, nondiscrimination, and fairness in dealing with people and groups. The laws and mandates are good, but they are limited in their ability to put into action God's mandate to love neighbor as self. The love coming from our hearts must come from the overflow of love from God to enable us to truly be good neighbors. Almost daily, we see and hear news of hate, discrimination, and crime committed by people against others, especially those different from themselves. The issue is only reported when the incident is obvious. But the dislike and distrust among people groups is real and growing. This is an elephant-in-the-room issue for many people. It is not often talked about publicly, but with all the poor neighbor relations taking place, our society is becoming more polarized with distrust, dislike, and

covert discrimination against those who differ from us in race and eth-
nicity. Poor neighbor relations breed social injustice and social unrest.
Such has really come to surface during this challenging time of the coronavirus pandemic.

We must find ways to overcome this as individuals and society. Why?
First, it is wrong; it flies in the face of God's commandment, "Love your
neighbor as yourself." Second, we are created unique and equal by God.
He did not create anyone better than another. Third, we Christians
need to recognize that when we all get to heaven, we will be coming
from every tribe, nation, and culture. We will be lovingly and continu-
ally praising and worshipping God without regard to race, language, or
nation. We should not wait. We should be praying and seeking God's
leading now to be the good neighbor He created us to be.

This is a heart issue that cannot be fully mandated by law. We must
do more to have compassion, love, and humble respect for those different from ourselves. This need is obvious. No one can make one love
a neighbor as self, but we need to acknowledge the need and start doing
more. Here is one possibility.

NATIONAL GOOD NEIGHBOR ORGANIZATION COULD HELP OVERCOME DISCRIMINATION

Just as the NAACP has done much to gain justice, fairness, and equal
rights for black people, there might also be a National Good Neighbor
Organization (NGNO). This could be focused on all neighbors and
advancing good neighbor relations among races, cultures, and ethnic
groups. Many would agree that we need to be better neighbors to those
different from ourselves; but as individuals, we are slow in making
progress here. Organized, we could lovingly and humbly encourage
each other to address this need, create awareness for the need, and get
involved to advance good neighbor relations while admonishing antagonistic acts that block good neighbor relations.

I would like to see an NGNO in every community with regular meetings, goals, structure, and activities. Each chapter needs to not just talk about good neighbor needs, but to be active daily, praying for neighbors and doing things for neighbors that not only provide help to those in need but also work together in compassion to strengthen bonds of love, care, and respect for each other. Lifting each other up just makes more sense than saying and doing things to pull others down and apart. A loving, organized group, using the Good Samaritan model, could have tremendous positive impact in inspiring all segments of society to, "Go and do likewise."

Each meeting could start with a prayer like this

Lord God, thank you for creating us to be in a loving relationship with you and our neighbors. Forgive us where we fail you in not being the good neighbor You mandated us to be. Help us to have compassion for all neighbors. Especially help us to put aside "self" and reach out to neighbors in need regardless of who they are. May they feel Your love through our kind acts.

Make us aware daily of opportunities where we can share Your love with neighbors. Give us courage to take actions of letting your love flow through us to any neighbor in need. Help us put aside any prejudice or hang-up that would block our being the good neighbors you command us to be. May our actions encourage many to, "Go and do likewise" and bring You the glory.

From the start, let each gathering focus on one or more wounded neighbor situations that need good-neighbor help. Prayerfully, get a plan and take action to meet that need. Once done, give God the glory.

An organized effort like this could do a lot to help heal the hurts and pains of social injustices and help bring unity among cultures, races, sexes, and religions. This need is too critical for us to ignore it or turn away "to the other side of the road." Please pray about how you might get involved or lead such a good neighbor effort in your community. For more information about starting or getting involved in a local NGNO in your community, see www.Loveyourneighborministries.com.

XII.

LET'S LOVE THE
DIFFICULT NEIGHBOR

B
eing a good neighbor requires reaching out to any neighbor in need. Some neighbors are open, kind, and receptive to receiving help. Some are somewhat indifferent but still receptive to receiving help or establishing neighbor relations. However, in many neighborhoods, there are some neighbors who are not only unreceptive to building bonds of trust, kindness, and respect, but also seem to go out of their way to be difficult and unlovable. Some of these neighbors are negative with just about everything, and some of them seem to be seeking ways to be offensive to their neighbors, especially those who do not share the same culture, economic status, race, religion, or social status.

There was one such character at my workplace from the Northwest USA. He was quick to condemn southern people for their language drawl and local customs and criticized and put down minorities and Hispanic immigrants. In addition, he could not engage in any conversation without profound cursing. Because he and I worked at the same office, it was necessary for us to interact on work-related activities. I made all-out efforts to avoid him, but there were times when I could not. One day, I asked him to refrain from the profound cursing in front of people at the workplace. My request just added fuel to the fire. He seemed to go out of his way with the cursing, knowing that I did not want to hear it.

If there was ever a difficult or unlovable neighbor, this guy had to be one. After some time, a thought came to me. I had a sign prepared and placed on the wall behind my desk. It read "Intelligent People Can Communicate Without Cursing." The next day he came to my office in a cursing outrage. He suddenly looked at the sign, his mouth froze, and he left immediately. Never again did I hear more than one or two curse words from him. Shaming him was not good, but the attention-getter worked.

Many of us have difficult neighbors. Being a good neighbor to difficult neighbors is not easy. But even they will have times of need. Such times can give us opportunities to show kindness, care, and respect, and to model Christ's love. What we must not do is to fight back with revenge, anger, display an antagonistic attitude, or lower ourselves to their level.

Most of us also have one or more neighbors who are not lovable, who do not want good neighbor relations for whatever reason. We cannot make these neighbors be good neighbors, but we can show kindness, respect, and care for them. By our being kind, respectful, and caring, they will know that they can look to us for help when they are in need.

The neighbor who appears difficult or unlovable is probably struggling with bad past neighbor experiences and probably needs a good neighbor relationship the most. Praying for them, modeling Jesus's love, and showing them compassionate care and respect can never hurt. Doing so can be a great step toward building a good neighbor relationship with them and helping them experience God's unconditional love for them.

XIII.

LET'S STAND IN THE GAP FOR THE UNBORN AND THE MOTHER

One of the most controversial issues in the US today is the "pro-choice" vs. "pro-life" stand regarding the unborn child. The "pro-choice" stand is that it is totally up to the expectant mother as to whether the unborn has a right to life. In stark contrast, there is the belief of many in society that the unborn is one of God's living creations, and though defenseless, has a right to life.

Pro-choice/family gives the expectant mother the right to decide if the unborn has a right to life. If she is not ready or prepared for children, if her health or life might be in jeopardy, if she is not ready to be pregnant or give birth, if the unborn might be unhealthy or abnormal, or if the pregnancy is the result of rape or incest, the "pro-choice" position says that the mother has the choice, not society, of deciding whether her unborn child has a right to life. Many in our society support this view and do not regard the unborn child having the right to life until birth.

Many "pro-life" people, in contrast, see the unborn child as a creation of God, a living, defenseless being, and the expectant mother with the privilege and responsibility for nurturing, protecting and giving birth to the baby. Many also believe that aborting or taking the life of the unborn is murder.

For many, treating the unborn as a neighbor is a complete turnoff. They do not regard the unborn child as having the right to life. Sad to say, much of our country's leadership has provided legislation to embrace this concept. This issue has created great division in our country. We live in a country where the far-left or the far-right politician can gain great support depending on the stance he/she takes on abortion. Personally, I do not see this as a simple black or white issue. While the mother is the instrument for bringing God's creation to new life, she in no way should be expected to give birth if she is a victim of rape or incest, or if the pregnancy jeopardizes her life. Being the instrument for birthing life, she does have the great opportunity, responsibility, and privilege of nurturing and protecting the new life. The father, too, has great opportunity, responsibility, and privilege for nurturing the new life by giving full support to the expectant mother through love, care, and financial support.

Society and neighbors also have a great opportunity, responsibility, and privilege for giving in many ways to encourage and support mothers and their developing babies who need nurture and care.

Sex is given to man and woman in marriage for the expression of intimate, sharing love and for beginning new life. Both man and woman should know that any intercourse could lead to pregnancy and new life. If they are not ready to start new life, they should take protective measures or not engage in intercourse. When honoring God in sexual relations, man and woman can have one of the greatest blessings of life—the giving of themselves to start a new life.

For many, treating the unborn as a neighbor in need of protection is a total turnoff; but here are some things that should be considered: (1) God is the creator of each life. His plan for each of us does not begin at birth; it begins even before were conceived. In Jeremiah 29:1-5 He says "before I formed you in the womb, I knew you, before you were born, I set you apart" (with a plan for your life). In Jeremiah 29:11, He says that plan is "to prosper you, not to harm you, to give you hope and a future."

For each life created, we parents and neighbors have responsibility to see that His plans are honored in the protection, nurture, birthing, loving and raising of children. (2) New life begins at conception. When the man's sperm (containing twenty-three chromosomes) unites with woman's egg (containing twenty-three chromosomes), life begins. Some big questions: Does the unborn baby have a right to life? If so, *when* does unborn have the right to life? Is it immediately after conception? Or is it after the first trimester, or after second trimester of pregnancy? Is it after the first heartbeat? Is it only after birth? Is it only if the baby is expected to develop into a normal, healthy human? Does the mother's health have first priority?

We can probably all agree that the beginning of new life is profound and precious, requiring great love, nurture, and care from man, woman, and society. But who can (or should) have the right to determine *when* the new life has a right to life? Does anyone outside the immediate family have any right to condemn or support the mother's rights as to whether she should accept and protect or reject the pregnancy? If the unborn is human life, does not a caring society have the right to defend the unborn? Can or should the unborn be considered a neighbor in need? If so, how should you and I respond?

The issue of "pro-life" versus "pro-choice" has strongly polarized our society. The extreme convictions as to when the unborn has right to life ranges from "any time after conception" to "no unborn has the right to life unless so given by the expectant mother." For me, I personally believe that life (any unborn) is a gift from God, and that every unborn child has a right to life, and that the expectant mother and father have the responsibility for protecting and nurturing that life. Having expressed this, I recognize that we live in a society where federal law gives the mother the right to decide whether or not to carry a pregnancy to term. For me, this seems hard to justify. Many believe the federal law should be overturned. With the great political divide in the US, that may not happen. Proposed legislation in several states is for human life to have the right to life from first heartbeat to the last. This view requires compromise on both sides. We as neighbors cannot ignore or look the other way on the issue of "right to life" for any of God's creation.

How, then, can we/should we reach out to be a good neighbor to the expectant mother? Here are some thoughts about what good neighbors can do regardless of their stance regarding "pro-life" or "pro-choice."

1- Like the Good Samaritan, we should have loving compassion for her. She needs to know, like Mary (Luke 1:38), that she is nurturing precious life created by God and that He already has a plan for that life, a plan to prosper and not harm it, and for it to have a future.

2- As a society, we need to care for her and her unborn and stand ready to help the expectant mother get any needed counseling, medical care, and financial support.

3- If she is not able to nurture and support the baby after birth, let her know that many couples unable to have children are eager to adopt and that there are organizations available to help make connections. Putting the expectant mother together with a couple seeking adoption might give the expectant mother encouragement to embrace and nurture the pregnancy.

The big questions for you and me are, are we willing to do more than talk about Pro-Life rights, and are we willing to give loving encouragement, give financial support, and/or adopt the precious newborn? Let us not be guilty of just condemning the "pro-choice" position but take loving action to encourage and support the expectant mother and let her know that we care for her and respect her decisions. For more information on ways to support, encourage and help unsure expectant mothers to appreciate and embrace the precious life she carries, see www. Loveyourneighborministries.com.

XIV.

LET'S HELP OUR
INCARCERATED NEIGHBORS

The number of people incarcerated in the USA has skyrock-
eted since 1980 (see figure below from US Bureau of Justice
Statistics).

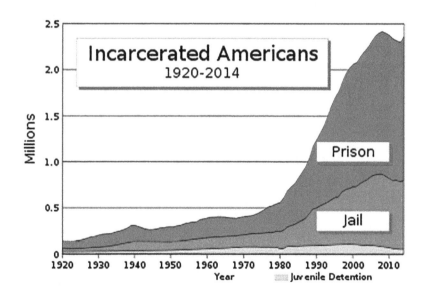

People in prisons and jails now total nearly 2.5 million. In addition,
there are nearly 5 million Americans on probation and parole from jails

and prisons. Over two-thirds of them are charged with or convicted of illegal drug use or trafficking. A prevailing attitude among many imprisoned is a sense of regret, failure, discouragement, rejection, and loss of hope because of past failures. Prison authorities, seeing this great need, are allowing for visitations and spiritual sharing. Every incarcerated person is a neighbor in need. They have a need for protection, legal assistance, a fair trial, and rehabilitation, but also for encouragement, forgiveness, and hope.

Currently, many prisons and jails allow for prison ministry. You and I need to see these as neighbors in need and seek God's leading as to how He can use us to be good neighbors to the incarcerated. You may think, "Wait a minute. They broke the law and they are getting their due punishment." Yes, each inmate charged or convicted is incarcerated because of legal issues, but they are still loved by God, and He still has a plan for their lives. God can use good neighbors to encourage them and help get them on the right path when released to a healthy, productive life of peace with Him.

Jesus had much to say about helping those in need, especially prisoners. In Matthew 25:35-40 (NIV), He said:

> For I was hungry ... thirsty ..., a stranger ..., needed clothes ... I was in prison and you came to visit me. Then the righteous will answer him, "Lord, when did we see you hungry ..., thirsty ..., a stranger ..., needing clothes ..., sick ..., or in prison and go to visit you?" The King will reply, "Whatever you did for the least of these brothers of mine, you did for me."

Jesus places the need for helping prisoners along with or just as important as helping all neighbors with needs, such as hunger, thirst, clothes, visitation, care, and so forth. Jesus did not command the release of prisoners but saw them as neighbors in need, especially for visitation, encouragement, and for letting them know or reminding them of God's unfailing love, care, and plan for them.

Okay, how can or should we be involved with these neighbors? First, know that many prisons and jails allow for ministry and/or visitation for inmates who are not on lockdown for whatever reason. Also, know that over half of inmates are receptive to some type of prison ministry.

At the Tift County, Georgia, jail, our sheriff and staff allow for jail ministry with necessary restrictions needed for inmates and volunteers. Anyone wishing to go into cell blocks to visit and share with inmates must comply with all state and local rules and guidelines. Volunteers must have approved background checks and take a training class to understand and follow rules in preparation for going into cell blocks to share with inmates. Anything to be given to inmates (Bibles, devotionals, books, reading materials, etc.) must be left with jail authorities for inspection and approval before passing on to inmates. After training, volunteers sign a waiver liability, assuming all risks for their involvement.

Inmates here in Tifton are usually given one to two opportunities for Bible study or "church" each week. They are also encouraged to set aside time daily for reading devotionals and the Bible.

At the Tift County Jail, separate church or Bible studies for male or females are held after the evening meal around 7:30 p.m. on Tuesdays and Thursdays. Guards announce that visitors are coming to share and request that the TV be turned off. Once inside, volunteers invite inmates to come join them in the dining area for a time of sharing, Bible study, and prayer. About half of the inmates usually come out to participate, many of them with their own Bibles. Many inmates are somewhat open about sharing their past failures, hurts, and hang-ups and express sincere desire for prayers and getting help for overcoming past failures when released.

As said earlier, Gersaid and I, along with other volunteers, make special efforts, in addition to sharing the Good News, to listen to them, encourage them, and point them to the abundant life in Christ they were created to have. In addition, we get for them (through the front office) Bibles, devotionals, and wholesome reading materials. Volunteers are instructed not to give anything to inmates directly other than their compassion and care for them. During sharing time, inmates are usually encouraged to make plans, once released, for walking in the light with godly people who can help them be encouraged and accountable to a legal, godly, good life. We also encourage them to not go back to the dark life of sin and self that trapped them and led to their incarceration.

If God touches your heart to help your incarcerated neighbors, here are some ways you might help.

- Get with your pastor or Sunday School class and organize jail ministry teams. There will need to be separate teams for male and female inmates. (You may want to develop special teaching materials for inmates. If not, the Bible studies used for your Sunday school class are usually good for sharing with inmates.)
- Let your sheriff's department know of your desire to minister to inmates. Ask if they are receptive and will arrange for training, background checks, and other needed instructions for ministry times and/or reading materials that can be made available for inmates. (Many inmates have poor vision. Most are not allowed to have glasses, so large- or giant-print reading materials are especially needed.)
- When sharing, do not just lecture to them; make special efforts to get their input for reading scripture, giving testimony, and praying. Share your testimony. Be an encourager and let them know of God's love and plan for their lives. Challenge them to have vision and a plan for walking in the light once released. Let them know of organizations like Celebrate Recovery that are available to help them once they are released. Encourage them to get connected with these and with a church family.
- Especially important is that you pray for them. Ask them about their prayer needs and concerns. When praying, make a special point to call them by name and let them know that God cares

for them. Invite them to pray the sinner's prayer if they have not already done so and let each one know that Jesus stands at the door ready to receive them.

- Follow all jail/prison guidelines for interaction with inmates. Some inmates will ask for special favors or to get messages to family and friends. If any request is not within the guidelines for lay ministers, ask them to make such requests through the prison authorities.

- Pray for God's protection and leading as you share with these neighbors. Give Him the glory for working in and through this ministry.

- Going inside jails and prisons is not a calling for everyone. But if you feel led and would like to learn more about getting directly involved see www.Loveyourneighbor ministries.com.

ADDENDUM 1

SOME PERSONAL EXPERIENCES IN GOING TO DOING LIKEWISE

WITH THE AFRICA INLAND CHURCH

Near the end of my career working as an agronomist for the University of Georgia Extension Service, I was invited by a pastor friend to help with an irrigation project in Tanzania along the shores of Lake Victoria, the world's second-largest freshwater lake. Jim, serving in Christian mission there, had observed that subsistence farmers were having more and more difficulty producing enough food for their families' survival. This was resulting from the Sub-Sahara Desert expanding east and south across Africa. Western Tanzania at one time had a three- to four-month rainy season, followed by dry months the remainder of the year. But that climate is changing; the rainy season is now becoming shorter and more erratic, making it difficult to plant, grow, and harvest a productive crop. Malnutrition and extreme poverty are becoming widespread.

My career had involved working with Georgia farmers to address their soil, water, and nutrient needs, especially for legumes. Jim approached me one day about going with him to Tanzania to observe their situation and work with him to develop a plan to help overcome the drought problem the farmers faced there. I received the invitation with joy, as I had a passion for helping improve farm productivity, especially for subsistence farmers. With much prayer, we prepared for the trip. Jim made all the travel arrangements in working with Bishop Peter Kitula, a leader in the African Inland Church (AIC). Our major objectives were to make assessments of the current soil nutrient and water needs near Lake Victoria and to work with AIC and government leaders to develop a practical plan for helping the village of Nytwali farmers irrigate from Lake Victoria. For this effort, I purchased a portable soil test kit to take on the trip.

The trip was a great enlightening experience for me. We flew to Nairobi, Kenya, then to Mwanza, and from there to Musoma, Tanzania where we met Bishop Kitula. There, he briefed us on the plans for the trip. We would lodge at the Lutheran Hospital in Bunda, and from there, work with church, government, and villagers to assess needs and to develop an irrigation plan to supply water to village gardens. Nytwali is located on the eastern shore of Lake Victoria, about ten miles north of Bunda. Helping meet the spiritual and physical need of Nytwali was a mission project for the Bunda African Inland Church.

Soils at Nytwali are part of the Serengeti Plain that extends from the north and east to Lake Victoria. We were there in February 1997. The rainy season, which usually began in December, had not come. Though appearing very dry, the landscape was beautiful, with scattered acacia trees.

At Bunda, we met with Charles Masale and other AIC leaders. They had arranged for Jim and me to meet with village leaders and Tanzanian government officials. Nytwali had about 500 residents. Most of the men were fishermen. They had small canoe-like boats and used nets to catch a variety of small fish. When we visited, they had the day's catch spread out and drying on the sandy lakeshore. After drying, some of the fish would be shared with the village and the remainder would be sold to nearby city markets.

After meeting with villagers and officials, we were taken to a fifty- or sixty-acre site that the villagers were using for food production. Beyond this area, there appeared to be 3,000 to 5,000 similar acres along the shores of Lake Victoria.

My first task was to determine the soil nutrient levels and needs of the area. I gathered soil samples, mixed them, and, using the portable test kit, did an analysis for soil pH, phosphorus, and potassium. To my amazement, the soil pH was near neutral (pH 6.5), which is good for most crops; the soil phosphorus and soil potassium levels were medium to high (also good for most crops). The soil texture appeared to be a sandy-clay loam. Everything about the test indicated that the area would be good for vegetable and crop production. Nitrogen and sulfur were the only nutrients testing low, and these could be supplied with a sulfur-based nitrogen fertilizer.

As the test results were shared with villagers, government officials, and church leaders, there was air of excitement about what could be produced on the land if plant water needs could be met. My pastor friend called for a time of prayer. He asked the group to hold hands and turned to me and said, "John, pray for the day that there will be center pivots watering this land and large articulating tractors plowing the fields."

I was spiritually overwhelmed at the request and said to him in front of at least fifteen people, "I can't pray that request, but I can pray for the empowerment of these people that they will get and learn to operate an irrigation system that will meet their current water needs." That I did. During the visit that day, I was silently praying, "God, how can we help these people in a way that they can help themselves and prosper?" Ironically, we all were standing close to a dilapidated, broken-down diesel irrigation pump that had been placed there by Israelis about thirty-five years earlier. It had been used for about ten years to supply water to the field. When it broke down, there was no one around to fix it. Parts of the motor had been removed, and the machine appeared inoperable at the time we were there. In my heart at the time was the feeling that if we were to be successful in helping these people meet their water needs, the help would have to be done in a way that would empower them so that they could help themselves, using local supplies, fuel, and equipment.

In order to do this, we would need to work in a way that would get them to take the lead and ownership of the project. My thoughts were that if we supplied everything and did everything to move water from the lake to the garden plots and did not involve them, that in a short time, our efforts would be no more successful than those of the Israelis thirty-five years earlier.

After we returned to our guest house at Bunda that night, my pastor friend began to quiz me about my response to him before the prayer that day. From his questions and comments, I could tell that I had offended him when he had called on me to pray before the group. We then talked for several hours about the kinds of basic irrigation technology and training that might be introduced that would be effective and inexpensive. We also explored how and where they might get local supplies. We talked a long time but had no good answers.

The last day there, we visited nearby Nassa Theological College. It was heartwarming to see about twenty students enrolled and living there with their families. Norm and Sheila Dilworth, American missionaries, working with the Africa Inland Mission, led the seminary training program that included several missionary instructors. Norm had acquired a tractor, farm equipment, and a tractor PTO pump for moving water from the lake for irrigating the rice and vegetable crops needed for the seminary staff and students. His success gave us confidence that similar success could be obtained at Nytwali. Before leaving Tanzania, we checked tractor and equipment prices at nearby Mwanza. Quoted prices were about three times the costs for the same items in the US. Diesel prices then were about $5.00/gallon. We were concerned that purchasing similar equipment might fail like the Israeli project had. We left Mwanza a bit discouraged, feeling that the cost of equipment, fuel, and maintenance would be quite high, but possible for the village.

Before leaving Tanzania, we made a commitment to Bishop Kitula and AIC leaders that we would return the next year with a mission team to set up a practical irrigation system for Nytwali. We also asked the AIC leaders to set the work effort up as part of a local evangelism ministry. They agreed to the request. We left Tanzania with the commitment to come back but did not know at the time how or what level of technology we would bring back for implementation. But God did.

On the return flight from Nairobi to Brussels, we continued to talk about the dilemma and what might be done to help the villagers meet their crop-water needs. While waiting in Brussels for the return flight to Atlanta, a professor from Emory University, who happened to be sitting in the plane seat in front of us, came and introduced himself. He said, "I was listening with much interest to your conversation and am wondering if you know about the treadle pump, a small two-cylinder manually-operated pump that can lift water up to twenty-five feet and supply up to ten gallons/minute." He explained that it was easy to build from leather and PVC pipe and that it was being used a lot in Southeast Asia. He also gave us a website that provided all the details and steps to building the pump. His estimate was that the pump without irrigation drip lines would cost no more than forty to fifty dollars. What he shared was divine. I immediately began looking into how the pump could be built and who God might lead to get involved with the next mission trip to Tanzania.

In the following months, I shared the Tanzania experience with church friends and anyone who would listen. I also sought information on how to build treadle pumps, materials needed for making treadle pumps, and getting together a manual to show people in Tanzania of how to make treadle pumps.

Shortly after returning to the US, my pastor friend came down with a serious illness, that, at best, would require months of recovery. He called to say that he needed to withdraw from going back on the second trip. I thanked God for his leadership which had introduced me to Tanzanian neighbors and their needs, and without reservation began to make plans to bring a mission team back to Tanzania in 1998.

As I shared the Tanzanian experience, I began recruiting men who might go on the second trip back to Tanzania and soliciting funds to help support the mission trip. The Fellowship of Christian Farmers helped with recruiting men and with fund-raising. The response and support were beyond belief. My father-in-law quickly gave $1,000 to support the return trip. A local friend and agricultural engineer, Tony Lastinger, took on the task of building three treadle pumps and committed to go to Tanzania to install them and to teach local agriculturists how to build and operate them.

My work associate at UGA and dear friend, Mike Beggs, also volunteered without reservation to go on the second trip. From the Fellowship of Christian Farmers publicity, Jim from Missouri and Dan from Ohio called, saying they wanted to participate. I had prayed for a five-man team to serve on the second mission. The commitment of these four men was an answer to prayer. Little did I know then how valuable a gift each man would bring to the second mission.

After the revelation about the treadle pump, men calling to participate, and support funds being raised, we contacted Bishop Kitula and AIC leaders and asked them to arrange the return trip with the purpose outlined below:

Our mission was:

1. Help prepare a site for Nytwali vegetable gardens.
2. Set up a treadle pump irrigation system for the site.
3. Demonstrate and teach how to operate the pump and make repairs.
4. Participate in a concurrent evening evangelism crusade, with one of the team giving testimony each evening.
5. Encouraging local church leaders

6. Providing some seeds, supplies, and funding for establishing garden plots, and

7. Growing in our spiritual journey from the experience.

The treadle pump looks somewhat like a stationary bicycle. It has two cylinders or pistons, one-way valves, and two spring-loaded pedals. Operation involved stepping alternately on the left and right pedals. As one pedal is pressed down, water is lifted (up to 25 ft.) and drawn into the cylinder. As the other pedal is pressed, water is drawn into it, and water from the first cylinder is released into a pipe that extends to drip irrigation lines in the garden area. One hour of pumping can supply and water a fifty- to seventy-five-foot garden area for two to four days.

The return trip was scheduled for February 1998, the beginning of the rainy season in Tanzania and a good time for planting garden plots. Our team from Georgia, Missouri, and Ohio met at the Atlanta airport. We flew from there to Nairobi, Kenya. There we took a five-man mission plane, just large enough to carry the team and our supplies to Musoma, Tanzania. AIC leaders then transported us to Bunda, Tanzania, our lodging headquarters and site for the evangelism crusade. The first weekend was spent getting with local AIC leaders and attending worship services at the Bunda AIC Church.

Our work mission was at Nytwali, about ten miles away on the banks of Lake Victoria. Bishop Kitula took us to Nytwali the first Monday morning to begin work setting up the irrigation system. Getting started turned out to be quite a challenge. Village leaders informed the bishop that they no longer wanted irrigation help or production assistance. Indian agri-business men had offered and paid them a good sum of money to lease 300 acres of land, including the five acres that was to be set up for garden plots. Although they had made a verbal commitment a year earlier to work with a mission team to establish an irrigation system for gardens, they had decided the rental cash offer of about $200 was too good to turn down.

Bishop Kitula refused to accept their statement. He spent two or three hours talking and negotiating with them, reminding them they had made a commitment for a mission team to come help them that February, and that the team was on site and ready to begin. The verbal scene appeared ugly at times with no breakthrough. Our team gathered under a nearby tree and prayed for a breakthrough. After about two hours, village leaders agreed to commit five acres for the garden plots.

This turned out to be only one of four challenges we faced. Just days before we arrived, a group of young boys were playing in the area and one was bitten by a ten-foot cobra and killed. Villagers were fearful of working in the four-foot-tall grass and weeds. The rains had come early that year. The grass and weeds were tall and had to be cleared before manual soil tillage could be done and irrigation drip lines could be installed ahead of vegetable planting. Setting up the irrigation system would take only about one day, but clearing the vegetation, hand tillage, and establishing irrigation drip lines for the four-acre area would take several days with lots of labor. Because of the cobra issue, hardly anyone wanted to work removing the tall vegetation. It was essential that the land be cleared and prepared and that the irrigation system be operational while we were on-site to show the villagers how to operate it if our mission was going to be successful.

The first workday, no one from the village came to help. Bishop Kitula went back to the village the second day to address the lack-of-help problem. What we were told was that the men of the village did not do garden work because that was a woman's job; they were fishermen. They did not want their women working with foreigners and still had great fear of the cobra known to be somewhere in the area. Bishop Kitula was unable to get the issue resolved that day.

We had come 8,000 miles to be good neighbors and to help these people with a critical food need. Was all the investment for naught? Our team was stunned but determined to get the area set up for productive garden plots. Tuesday through Saturday that week, we got up early each day, were transported to the site, and worked intensively weeding and tilling. Days 1–9, no one from the village came to help. We only took short breaks for water and lunches that were prepared for us by the church leaders back at Bunda.

We knocked off work about 4:00 p.m. each day and returned to Bunda to shower, dress, and participate in an evening evangelism crusade. This was an "open air" event set up on the main street of Bunda. One of our team gave his testimony each night. A church leader then translated the testimony into Swahili. Two to three hundred people gathered each night for participation. Each evening was a wonderful experience, with lots of lively praise songs and profound preaching. Each service ended with a call for salvation or a rededication of life. Scores of people came forward each night to be led in prayer to receive Jesus as Savior and Lord. During the five-day crusade, over 200 people came forth to make a profession of faith or to rededicate their lives to serving Jesus. To be a part of something so profound and life-changing made our mission team feel so blessed, even though we were struggling to get the villagers involved and empowered to meet their critical water need.

Each day we prayed for a breakthrough for being able to communicate and work with the Nytwali villagers. This would be essential for getting the garden plot irrigation system set up and operating. With only two workdays left, we arrived at the site and saw forty or fifty villagers there to meet us. All had hand tools and had come to help with tillage. We were overwhelmed with gratitude and thanked God for the breakthrough.

By the end of the day, all the planned garden plots were prepared for planting and set up with irrigation drip lines. Tony gave instructions on how to operate the treadle pumps. Several young men began practicing the pump operation. We left Nytwali that day deeply touched for the experience, not just for giving, but for having helped to empower this village to help themselves with their critical need for water. As we were getting ready to leave, the village chief and several others came to us and gave our team a special gift, a large black goat. We graciously thanked them, not knowing what we should do with the goat. Our driver took the goat, tied it to the top of our transport vehicle, and brought it back to Bunda with us. We were then told that there would be a special going-away celebration banquet for us at the Bunda AIC Church. The goat would provide the main meat dish. It was a joyful occasion! We were deeply touched by the kindness, hospitality, care, and affection extended to us by the local church.

We returned home grateful and joyful for the experience of trying to be good neighbors, and for not just giving, but working in ways to encourage and empower the people of Nytwali. One of our team, Dan from Ohio, was so touched by the trip that he went back that summer to help the villagers with the irrigation system and other production needs for the garden plots.

With Agricultural Leaders in Bangladesh

During most of my career, I worked as a Soybean Production Specialist for the University of Georgia, advising county extension office personnel and farmers on the latest research and best methods for growing soybeans. After retirement in 1998, I was invited by USAID to assess soybean production challenges in Bangladesh and to develop guidelines for them for improving soybean productivity there. They needed help at that time. They were producing only sixteen to eighteen bushels of soybeans per acre, less than half of the US average per-acre yield.

The assignment was to be for two months. My assignment was to first visit soybean fields in all parts of the country to assess production needs and problems that limited soybean productivity there. Afterward, I was to prepare a comprehensive report and present the findings to agricultural leaders before returning to the US.

I eagerly accepted the invitation, thinking that God could use my expertise to help these neighbors with critical food/protein needs. At that time, Bangladesh (area about two-thirds that of Georgia-USA) had 127 million people. Quality diet and protein nutrition were critical needs, especially for growing children. I had been told that use of treadle pumps and portable one-cylinder diesel engine pumps were common there. After the Tanzanian experience, I was also eager to learn about how effective these irrigation systems were there, and if in learning, I might gain additional information to share with the Tanzanians.

When I arrived at Dhaka, Bangladesh, it was Ramadan, and the senior agronomist with whom I was to work was on a pilgrimage to Mecca. The USAID leader there asked me to remain at the guest house through the last week of Ramadan and then to begin field studies with Asad, the leader's assistant. I was eager to get started, but for my safety, it was necessary not to be out in public at that time. The week seemed to pass so slowly. I paced the room often, read lots of scripture and the national newspaper (English version) daily. CNN was the only English channel on TV. I watched it a lot to keep up with world news. The Dhaka paper had lots of local and world news events on the front page. But on the next several pages each day, editors trashed the US, Britain, and most other Western countries as evil and bad.

On Easter Sunday, I received word that the field survey work would begin on that day. I was disappointed that I was called to begin work then. But I had already spent several hours reading and rereading the Easter stories, and taking my quiet time to thank God for His love that poured out so graciously the first Easter. During the quiet time, I was reminded often of His love, so great that He had sent His Son to the cross so that I (and all mankind) might have atonement and a restored relationship with Him. I had come to Bangladesh not only to offer help for soybean production needs, but also to look for ways to share the good news of Easter. I wore a white sports shirt that day as a statement for Easter, hoping that someone might ask, "Why the white shirt?"

Three men came to pick me up that Easter morning. They gave introductions that we would begin surveying fields in the southern areas of Bangladesh and work our way to the northern area in the next five or six weeks. We rode in a small boat about forty miles down the Brahmaputra River to start the survey work. They did ask me about the white shirt. This gave me time to share my faith in response to their questions.

The older gentlemen did not like what I had to say. He insisted that I find time to learn and worship Allah. The young assistant, Asad, though, was kind and asked lots of questions about Christianity. This trip set the stage for Asad and I to become good friends, and for him to develop an interest in Christianity, an interest that later, sad to say, caused him to be demoted and punished. We met our Jeep driver down the river near Chittagong and began field surveying late that Easter Sunday.

That evening, we drove to a Mennonite NGO guesthouse for dinner and lodging. These Brazilian Mennonites had introduced soybeans to Bangladesh. They had one variety superior to all others in seed quality, but one that was slightly marginal in yield. Their faith mission there appeared to be incognito and very subtle. They had established a soybean research farm at the site. The next day we studied their field plots before beginning field surveys.

For the next five weeks, Asad and I traveled and walked soybean fields (usually one to two acres in size), making assessments. We took soil and leaf samples that would be later taken to a material lab for analysis. We rated plants in field for diseases, nematodes, or other abnormalities. A USAID jeep driver was assigned to the project to get us from one site to another. The journey took us all the way from Chittagong to the Indian border. The five weeks traveling and working with Asad gave me the opportunity to really get to know him and to share my Christian testimony with him. The experience also gave me opportunity to learn about the Bangladeshi people, their needs, and culture.

The daily routine was an interesting experience for me. We lodged at very spartan guest houses, at experiment station guest quarters, and in homes. We ate at least two meals a day in local restaurants. The setup was similar at each restaurant. Most had, at the entrance, a wash station with several faucets. The main dining room was for men only. If women came, they and their party had to go to a side entrance, totally separated from the main dining room. The dining experiences were unlike anything I had ever had before. The main dish was usually sticky rice served with a very spicy meat/vegetable curry. There were no forks, knives, or spoons. Diners would take the rice and squeeze or roll it into a tight ball and dip it into the curry. Asad informed me that you always use your right hand for dipping and eating, and that you always use your left hand for wiping.

I had never eaten sticky rice and curry before with my hands. So, after the first meal, I asked Asad to find me a fork, which he did as we went through a nearby village. I also learned after the first meal to pick the tiny peppers out of the curry as I ate. I love spicy foods, but those little things were so hot that they literally took my breath away. After work hours, and while traveling, Asad and I talked a lot about religion and issues of faith. He was Muslim and shared how important it was to do good works and to give to the poor to honor God. Giving to the poor was an important issue there, as the most Bangladeshi people are poor. They worked hard to earn very little; most earned just enough income to meet basic life needs. Many were homeless and lived on the streets of Dhaka. Asad said that a common belief there was that if the poor worked hard, honored their master, and did good, that after death, they would be reborn to life at a higher status.

Asad became very curious and interested in my faith and testimony. I shared my testimony with him and that my relationship with God was through confession of my sins, praying for forgiveness, and trusting Jesus as Savior and Lord. I shared with him Ephesians, Chapter 2, that salvation comes through faith, not from being good or anything that one can do to earn it or boast about what one has done. I shared with him that we are God's workmanship, created in Christ to do good work. I went on to share with Asad that my coming to Bangladesh was out of my desire to let God use my expertise to do good works, to help Bangladesh improve its food and protein quality, to help meet a critical physical need. I also shared that my being there was, in a small way, giving back to God for the great gift of eternal life given to me. Helping the poor, I shared, had always been a passion of mine. I told him about the US Peace Corps established by President John Kennedy and that I had considered joining the Peace Corps to help people in developing countries with food production.

I also shared my Tanzania experience and their ongoing challenge with drought, and our team efforts to help them develop effective, low-cost irrigation systems. We both agreed that helping others in need was a good thing, regardless of faith background.

Near the end of the travel and field evaluations, we saw one farmer using a small, one-cylinder diesel irrigation pump to draw water from a small pond. He was irrigating about one acre of crops and vegetables. I was impressed, thinking that this might have potential for helping Tanzanians with their need for advancing irrigation there. We asked questions but could not learn where the pump was made. The pump had been given to the farmer. Asad thought that it either came from India or China. He knew an agricultural engineer working in Dhaka, who might know, and said he would arrange a trip for us to visit him when we returned to Dhaka.

When our field studies were finished, arrangements were made for us to fly back to Dhaka. After getting dropped off at the airport, we had about a three-hour wait before boarding for the return. While waiting, four nuns dressed in habits came in and sat in seats across from us. Asad took notice of these and asked me who would be wearing such clothing. I was surprised that he did not recognize them as nuns. I told Asad,

"These are nuns." Several questions followed: "Why are they here? What are Catholics? Where are they from? What do they believe?"

I asked Asad if he knew about Mother Teresa and the Pope. He did and I said that they were both Catholic. I didn't know a lot about Catholics but told him that the nuns were deeply devoted and committed to a life of celibacy, deeply devoted to worshipping and serving God, and deeply devoted to helping people in need. I went on to say that they were probably serving God like Mother Teresa, helping poor Bangladeshi families with food and/or health needs. Asad was touched that the nuns were giving so much of themselves to help the poor.

After getting back to Dhaka, we took the plant and soil samples we had collected to a lab for analysis. During the next two weeks, I spend much of the time writing a report summarizing our field observations. Asad also arranged a seminar so that a summary report of the findings and recommendations could be presented to national agricultural leaders.

He had become interested in my desire to get information on sources for the one-cylinder irrigation pump and followed up on arranging a visit for me to meet with the agricultural engineer and irrigation specialist. The engineer had received a PhD at the University of Minnesota several years earlier. When Asad and I met with the engineer, he seemed receptive to the inquiry until I mentioned that I was working with the Africa Inland Church on a special water needs project. At that point, he became enraged, saying that under no circumstances would he offer any help to a Christian church mission. Then he got up and left.

Asad and I were both stunned at his response. Both of us had the same thought, "How could a man given a special scholarship and training in the US not have a heart for giving back to help poor subsistence farmers in Africa because of religious differences?" I gained no insight on where or how to purchase the special irrigation pumps while in Bangladesh, but the encounter set the stage for Asad and me to have an in-depth discussion about giving. He and I both agreed that helping one in need was the only right thing to do regardless of whether they were like us or not. It also opened the door for me to share with Asad that a basic tenet of the Christian faith was giving in love in response to what was first given in love from God, the Father. I cited several scriptures about His love for us and His command for us to, "Go and do likewise." In the following days, I was overwhelmed by Asad's efforts to give gifts to me, including custom-made shirts, a silk tie, and his taking me out to eat at a nice Thai restaurant in Dhaka.

Asad shared anguish that he and his wife were not yet able to conceive and have children. I told him that I would pray that God would open the door and open it soon. He expressed much gratitude. Then, the next day, he asked me if I would come with him after work that day and offer up a prayer for him and his wife to have a child. That I did, and I told him that God, at the right time, would make that possible. My prayer now is that all prayers in this regard were answered.

The evaluation report was completed in the eighth week. No major disease or fertility problems were found. The three most significant soybean problems observed were stunted growth, drought, and poor stands due to poor seed quality. The overall problem was that Bangladeshi farmers were trying to grow a summer-adapted crop during winter and spring months. Bangladesh has a somewhat tropical climate that would permit or allow for fair to good soybean growth during the winter/spring period. But most soybean varieties are long day photo-period-sensitive plants best suited to spring/summer plantings. There are some near day-neutral varieties, but most of the higher-yielding varieties are day/night-length-sensitive and are best suited to spring/summer plantings.

The big problem for trying to grow soybeans during the summer period in Bangladesh is that it is the monsoon season (mid-May through early September) when daily rains occur. Trying to plant, grow, and harvest soybeans during this time is extremely challenging there. Most of Bangladesh is semi-tropical with rather mild winters and springs. With this climate, they were having some success planting soybeans in December and planting early maturing varieties that matured by late April. But planting in December when soil temperature was fifty to sixty degrees Fahrenheit often resulted in poor seed emergence, especially if seed quality was weak. The longer winter nights caused the plant stunting, and the increasing day length in spring had a negative impact on fruit set and caused non-uniform maturity. The spring periods were often dry, adding further stress to growth and yield.

Asad set up a national workshop for me to share this information. The response to my sharing was mixed. Some thought that their problems could be mostly resolved if their farmers just quit growing the Mennonite soybean variety. They wanted me to put into the report that the Mennonite variety should not be recommended. That I would not do, because of all varieties planted, it had the best growth and seed quality for the winter-spring culture period. I stressed that getting improved seed quality was much needed and that they also needed to seek improved harvest and storage conditions to get planting seed with acceptable germination and seed vigor. I also recommended they seek getting more day-neutral varieties with known high-seed vigor, and they further look at planting the late-maturing varieties that could be planted before the summer monsoon season, and varieties that did not mature until after dry weather began in late September. After returning to the US, I did procure and send them soybean seed of two very late-maturing varieties that might have potential for late spring-summer planting.

I left Bangladesh with lots of mixed emotions: (1) How could I have been a better neighbor? (2) Should I have been bolder in sharing my faith? (3) Should I have defended Western countries for supporting Israel? (I chose to say nothing, other than I know of no one who hates Bangladesh and that everyone I know wants to see the needs of Bangladeshi people be met). (4) For the engineer who refused to give help for getting information on sources for irrigation pumps sought by the African Inland Church, I did not challenge him. Should I have expressed appreciation for his concerns, or should I have reminded him that people of different cultures and religions willingly supported him as he sought higher education? (5) For the agricultural leaders who wanted the Mennonite soybean variety not grown, I did offer defense because it was superior to other grown varieties in seed quality. Was there a better way to address their concerns?

I did come away from the experience seeing culture and religion strongly influencing leaders' decisions sometimes in ways that did not help get top-yielding-quality soybeans. Asad's seeing through some of these problems was a blessing for me. Asad communicated later that he had been demoted. He did not say why but probably related to his not supporting other decisions and recommendations.

HELPING CHINESE STUDENTS IMPROVE CONVERSATIONAL ENGLISH

Ina and I had the privilege of going to China four times to help Chinese college students with conversational English and to share our Christian faith. We found the Chinese people we met everywhere to be kind, respectful, loving, beautiful, and passionate for improving their education and quality of life. In a sense, I was a tag-along as my wife was skilled teaching and speaking English. We both had a passion for modeling and sharing our faith with Chinese students.

Our first trip there was to Nanchong in the summer of 2003. Arrangements had been made the prior December for us to go there with ten others. Shortly after we committed to go to China, the SARS epidemic broke out there. International travel was halted for about four months. Our sponsor kept the team posted, and in late March, sent word that they would release any team member who wanted to withdraw. After prayer, my wife and I said, "No, we don't want to withdraw." We felt led of God to go; if He called us to go, then we would look to Him for guidance and protection for going to China if international travel opened there before summer. It did in mid-May, and we began rapidly making plans to get our plane reservations. Of the twelve people committed to China to teach conversational English, only we and Mr. Jack from Texas went to China.

We were told that Chinese students were well-trained throughout grade school years in the basics of English but lacked ability to converse well with the English-speaking world. Our challenge was to develop interactive conversational settings where we would give brief lectures that included scripts with keywords and phrases. For response, the class would be divided into teams that would verbally respond with questions. Classes were structured with students being assigned to a team of four or five. Each class would usually have four to six teams. After the instruction, students were given opportunities to ask questions and inquire about American life relative to the subject. The team response was structured in ways to get every student speaking one or more impromptu sentences each day. It worked well. As they gained confidence, they began asking lots of questions about the subjects and our lives in America. Both we and the students learned a lot about each other and developed a deep love, care, and respect for each other and our respective countries.

In the classrooms, our subjects focused on American holidays: Thanksgiving, Christmas, Valentine's Day, and Easter. As Christians, we were able to give testimony to the importance of these days to our own lives. We were told not push our faith on the students but that we could freely give Christian testimony in response to questions asked relative to our faith. In the beginning, some students boasted that they had no religious beliefs, but after six to ten days of sharing, most of the classes would ask lots of questions about Christianity and wanted to get English/Chinese Bibles (that were available at state churches).

Getting to know, understand, and appreciate Chinese neighbors was one of the greatest experiences of our lives. Ina and I encountered a whole new, different, and special world. Overall, we met kind, respectful, intelligent, loving, and seeking people. Kindness and hospitality were wonderful beyond anything we expected. Students were generally eager to learn. They not only attended classes with much interest but were eager to take us to their homes, to nice restaurants, and to tourist sites of interest. They gave us several special gifts; some included special china from generations past.

Their work ethic was so impressive. Construction was ongoing everywhere. It appeared that China was rapidly moving from a populous, developing country to an economic powerhouse. Many cities were huge, with 10-plus million people.

Our Chinese students showed great interest in our Christian sharing. We did not try to directly evangelize but found most students eager to go to registered churches with us and eager to receive Bibles that were available at the state churches. We actually had one student ask, "What must I do to have a relationship with Jesus?" Getting to share the Good News with students in and out of class was a great joy and blessing.

We saw China as a great country with opportunities moving toward an advanced economy, and also, a country with great food, housing, transportation, health, environmental, and spiritual needs. It was encouraging to see so many people exercising when walking or biking to and from work and other activities.

Two obvious problems observed were heavy air pollution in and around large cities and a high number of men smoking tobacco. The smog around several cities appeared to be associated with air inversion and were magnified by coal burning and heavy traffic. It appeared that nearly half the men on the street were smokers. My guess is that increases in wages were giving them enough income to buy and get addicted to tobacco. That addiction will likely lead to lung cancer becoming a major health issue in China.

After four summer trips to China, Ina and I came away with deep love, care, and respect for our Chinese neighbors who showed us compassion, love, and respect. Yes, they are working hard to advance themselves and their society. Yes, there are differences between their society's leadership and ours. But for the world community, China has much to offer in the way of affordable prices for many, many products. China has lots of needs for food, feed, technology, and services. Our prayers are that US, world, and Chinese leaders will work together to help each other in positive ways and to help each other meet needs. We need each other as good neighbors. Pulling together as good neighbors and looking out for each other certainly seems more logical than generating tariffs and other restrictions. Advancing good neighbor relations between the US and China should be encouraged. It is much needed, especially in ways that promote fair trade, respect for intellectual property rights, and human rights.

We humbly thank our newfound Chinese friends for their friendship and for showing us much about their culture and beautiful country. We must work together to improve good neighbor relationships between our two great countries.

WORKING TO HELP EMPOWER
HAITIAN NEIGHBORS

One of the poorest, most struggling countries in the Western Hemisphere has to be Haiti. The country has been devastated by hurricanes, corrupt leaders, major earthquakes, hunger, and health issues.

The central highlands of Haiti were once tropical rainforests. Much of this area now has severely eroded infertile slopes with limited potential for food production and/or reforestation. Looking down from space, the eroded hills stand in stark contrast to the adjoining forests of the Dominican Republic. The heavy deforestation and tree removal for charcoal production and lumber has left these steep hills bare and vulnerable to erosion. This has occurred repeatedly as tropical storms and hurricanes have swept across these lands. There is a critical need for vegetating and reforesting these hills, not only to protect these lands, but also to help meet current food and wood product needs.

To add to Haiti's struggle, a magnitude 8.5 earthquake stuck Port-au-Prince and nearby areas in 2010. Many lives, homes, and properties were destroyed. The UN and many charitable organizations rushed in with immediate help to provide shelter, food, and basic needs for Haitian families. Literally thousands of tent homes were erected in and around Port-au-Prince. The tent cities provided shelter, safe food, water, and toilet facilities. The immediate needs of thousands were met.

Progress in getting Haiti restored and strengthened to be self-sustaining has been challenging. Funds and supplies for rebuilding housing and infrastructure have been limited. Five years after the earthquake, most tent cities were still fully occupied, providing better facilities for poor people than what they had before the earthquake. Our Haitian neighbors are still in much need of empowerment so that they can begin to fully recover and grow beyond their struggles. As neighbors, we can and should do more to help guide them to ways of empowerment.

One critical need in Haiti is adequate quality protein, especially for growing children. Many children there show the characteristic swollen belly symptoms of malnutrition. How to help empower Haitians to meet these needs became a challenge for the US, the Episcopal Church, NGOs, the University of Georgia, and Fort Valley State University. Graham Huff with the League of Hope worked with these organizations to get a team plan for helping meet these critical food needs. Since I had research experience working with forages and vegetating infertile highway slopes, I was invited to participate and explore ways that forages could be established on the barren hills for goat browsing

Two approaches were explored: (1) increasing goat milk and meat production, and (2) increasing peanut production for making peanut butter and high protein/energy nutrition snacks.

For increasing meat and milk production, the focus was on improving goat production. Goat was the preferred meat animal choice because most land holders had only one-half to one acre of land, not enough to sustain a single cow. In the central highlands of Haiti, boys daily took the family herds to nearby hills and slopes so that the goats could browse and feed on shrubs, weeds, and other plants. Unfortunately, many of the slopes and hills are highly eroded and infertile, with little vegetation.

FVSU animal scientists conducted seminars to train Haitian agricultural leaders on ways to reduce stomach parasites. This involved improved grazing management and introduction of new breeds of goats with parasite resistance.

I was invited to join the team to explore ways to improve forage quality and quantity, especially on the eroded slopes. My involvement started by taking soil samples and making assessments as to which forage plants and management practices might be used to improve productivity. This task became quite a challenge; the soils were not only highly eroded, but also were low in potassium and phosphorus. The eroded soils did have a near neutral soil pH which is good for most plants. I had a vision that *Sericea lespedeza* might be good for these slopes and for goats. Here in the US, goats love to browse this legume. The tannins in *Sericea lespedeza* leaves are known to reduce stomach parasites. I was also interested in trying *Sericea lespedeza* there because it is a long-lived perennial legume somewhat tolerant of low soil fertility and low pH. I took *sericea lespedeza* seed to Haiti in 2014 to establish research plots with varying seeding and fertility rates. These were established to assess the potential of this legume there.

I returned in 2015 to help agricultural leaders set up test plots to help evaluate the potential of the *Sericea lespedeza* for establishment on central highland slopes. Haitian agricultural leaders were very cooperative in locating land for the test plots and in getting supplies together to conduct the tests. Establishing plots with soil scarification and fertility treatments, ranging from nothing to high, went well. Before returning to the US, I requested that a fence be erected around the area to keep animals out. This was necessary as *Sericea lespedeza* requires two to three years to become established and tolerant to defoliation. Commitments were made to do so. We were to get back together one year later for follow-up, to see if there were differences in treatments for successful establishment.

We did get back together the next year to evaluate plots, but with much disappointment. No fence had been erected to protect the *Sericea lespedeza*. What we found was that every plot had been grazed to the ground and there was no way to rate the plots to determine whether any of the treatments were successful. This chapter closed for me about where it started. The central highlands of Haiti still have need of permanent low-cost, low-maintenance forages. *Sericea lespedeza* may or may not be of great value for helping meet this need, but it and other forages must be further explored.

The team working to increase protein needs with peanuts had a more successful story. The UGA team was able to identify several adapted peanut varieties and establish production guidelines for Haitian farmers. Peanut production in the valleys has now increased significantly and a US business joined the effort in building a small peanut processing plant. Quality nutritional snacks are now becoming available for Haitian children. This initiative, if further expanded, offers great potential for helping empower Haitian farmers and to meet nutritional needs for Haitian children.

As for my involvement, I struggled with the question: "What should Haitian agricultural leaders do to help small subsistence farmers, ranchers, and shepherds there increase hillside forage production for goats?" Hopefully, they will further explore the ideas we tried. Should financial support be given to them for exploring possibilities, or should the UN, NGOs, and charities take on major efforts themselves to revegetate central highland slopes? If Haitian food/protein needs are to be met, their leaders must take ownership of the empowering process. I see it as a great challenge for them, but not impossible.

Sharing with Cuban Neighbors

US Cuba relations deteriorated after Cuba turned to communism in 1960. Castro made a major effort to denounce Christianity and closed most of the churches there. He largely blamed the church for creating upper, middle, and poor classes of society. The US and much of the world criticized Castro for taking away religious liberty and freedom from the people of Cuba. However, as Castro aged, he appeared to be less threatened by the church and began to ease up a bit on religious worship after the year 2000. He did not allow people to return to large church buildings but did allow for house churches that had twenty-five or fewer participants. Doing so provided a great mission field for Rob and Sandy White, Cletus and Marveena Lynch, and others to take mission teams to Cuba and work with local Christian leaders to help establish house churches.

In the winter of 2003, Rob White came to my church, announcing this mission opportunity and making an appeal for Christians to join him and his wife, Sandy, to go on a mission trip to Cuba that year. Without reservation, I accepted Rob's invitation to go to Cuba with them. When I shared team plans with my father-in-law, Bloise Zeigler, he immediately said, "I want to go, too." I was amazed at his interest and enthusiasm to get involved; he was ninety years old at the time of joining the team but had remarkably good mental and physical health for his age.

The 2003 mission was to include nurturing and supporting existing house churches, conducting backyard Bible studies, participating in street evangelism, teaching and preaching in house church worship services, helping establish one or more new house churches, and participating in Gulf of Mexico baptisms for new converts. Each time our leader, Rob, met with Cubans, he made a point to tell them, "I/we love Cuba, I/we love Cubans." The Cubans responded, showing much love and appreciation for our mission team. Great friend and neighbor relationships were established that lasted long after the trip.

I had long coveted improved relations with Cuba. A Cuban family had visited my church in the late 1950s. They were wonderful people with a beautiful spirit. After the revolution, we never saw them again. It did not seem right for loving, kind neighbors to be separated because of drastic differences in the governing policies of our two countries, so my heart's desire was to go modeling Christ's love and to show good-neighbor respect to Cubans. In five trips to Cuba as part of mission teams, I came also to have compassion, love, and respect for Cuban people and to learn of their thirst for spiritual renewal. At the time Castro overthrew the Batista government, many Cuban Christians were forced to withdraw from any participation in corporate worship and were persecuted if they did not.

My first trip there in 2003 was most dramatic for me. Our team of twelve Christians from South Carolina, Tennessee, Georgia, California, and Alabama assembled at the Miami airport. Rob White briefed everyone on the things to do and not do in respecting the government there. At that time, it was not possible to travel directly to Cuba because of government restrictions. To get to Havana, we flew to Jamaica, got visas, and then got a flight to Havana. We found Havana to be a very attractive city, reminiscent of the US in the 1950s. There we saw many 1950s-era US cars on the streets. It was amazing to see how well they had been maintained and kept in operating condition. Our trip had been coordinated with Roberto, a minister there, who provided leadership for house church establishment. He had permission from the Cuban government to organize house churches, consisting of no more than twenty-five persons per house. Each house church was structured to have a pastor, usually bi-vocational, and a worship music leader. Participants met two or three times weekly for fellowship, Bible study, prayer, and worship.

Our mission was to support and encourage the house church groups. We were to participate in street evangelism for sharing the good news of Christianity and to help establish new house churches.

For the first trip, I was given the assignment of street evangelism with Rob's wife, Sandy. It sounded good, but as I stepped out on the street that first day, I was nearly overcome with fear. I thought, *This is Communist Cuba. I'm about to get arrested and imprisoned for sharing the Gospel.* Then, I was convicted as the thought came: *How childish and immature can I be? Your neighbor needs to know God's love for them, and His plan of redemption for them is far greater than any need I might have for protection from the Cuban government.* I was then reminded of Romans 1:16 (I am not ashamed of the gospel ...), and 2 Timothy 1-8 (Do not be ashamed to testify about our Lord ...). I did pray for protection and that nothing would hinder our calling and mission there.

My heart was deeply touched and filled with joy as we made street contact with Cubans. We had been assigned a young Cuban woman to translate for us. She was not only passionate for Jesus but was also fluent in English.

One of our first street contacts was a young girl, between twelve and fourteen years old. After Sandy shared God's love and plans for her, she then gave her an invitation to trust Jesus as Lord and Savior. The young girl became tearful, and without hesitation, she prayed the sinner's prayer for salvation. Sandy then gave her some Christian tracts for Bible study and Christian growth. I was overjoyed to see how God worked in and through this encounter. My fear of being on a Cuban street had largely disappeared by this time.

On the second day, Sandy, our interpreter, and I started out walking to meet some people on the street and to visit some who had shown interest in becoming part of a church group. Within a block, we met the young girl that Sandy had led to the Lord the day before. She asked if we would come to her home to pray for her father who had severely injured his back in a work accident. We got to their house and were met by her mother at the door. She invited us in and introduced us to her husband who was lying flat on a sofa. He told us about his accident; while in helping lift a heavy load of material with others, the weight suddenly shifted to his side and this had left him with severe back pain. He had not received any medical treatment but was sent home, treated only with aspirin. I shared scripture about God's power for healing through prayer and His desire for us to call on Him in time of need. Before prayer, we asked if he knew and trusted Jesus as Lord and Savior. The father said he did not. Sandy shared scripture with him and asked him if he would like to come to know Jesus as Lord and Savior. He said he would! I then turned to his wife and asked her the same question. She responded yes, also. We then laid hands on them and prayed for his healing and their salvation. They appeared deeply touched. All of us, including the interpreter, teared up with joy seeing their response. We gave them a New Testament and scripture tracts and then continued with other visits. We humbly thanked God that day for letting us be good neighbors to a family with both physical and spiritual needs.

Two young men from our mission group, firefighters from California, conducted baseball camps every day for teenage boys. Their mission was to teach baseball-playing skills and to share Jesus. It was obvious that young Cuban men loved baseball as many youngsters turned out for the camps every day. Our young firemen dressed for outdoor sports, wearing shorts and T-shirts.

All of the team members had been told to keep passports on them at all times. The young firemen broke this rule one day, leaving the passports in the hotel room because they lacked a place to keep them with their sports dress. It appeared that Cuban authorities were monitoring our activities because Cuban soldiers came to the house church that day and asked to see our passports. The two young firemen were not able to present them. They were detained for several hours until someone could go to our hotel, about fifteen or twenty miles away, and get their passports. The soldiers also said that it had been reported that the number of people at the house church exceeded the allowed number of people at a gathering. Some of us had been late returning for lunch that day. When the soldiers went into the house church to count heads, they found that there were exactly twenty-five people there, the maximum allowable limit for a gathering. The events of that day were disconcerting, but our mission team went on with our planned activities with the blessings and protection of God.

We shared backyard Bible studies and evangelism messages daily. People attending were usually some of the house church members, plus others who had been invited to the gathering after being contacted through street evangelism. Near the end of our mission, David, a member of our team, shared a powerful evangelistic message and then extended an invitation for people to respond. Four or five people accepted Jesus as Lord and Savior. I was sitting in the back row that day when the invitation was extended. I noticed that the woman next to me began to cry but did not respond to the invitation. I called an interpreter and asked if she would ask the woman if she would like to accept Jesus as her Lord and Savior and if she would let me share the plan of salvation with her. The tearful woman said, "Yes!" We gave her a Spanish Gideon New Testament that had the plan of salvation on the back two pages. The interpreter shared the scripture, telling her, "God loves you" (John 3:16), "all are sinners" (Rom, 3:23; 3:16), "God's remedy for sin" (Rom. 6:23; John 1:12; 1 Cor. 15:3-4), and "all can be saved now" (Rev. 3:20; Rom. 10:13). After making a profession of faith, the woman became joyful. We had her sign the New Testament, saying that she had received and trusted Jesus as her Savior.

As our mission trip concluded, a baptism service was set up in the nearby Gulf of Mexico for the thirty-five to forty people who had made professions of faith. I was asked to baptize the young woman that we led to the Lord at the backyard Bible study and I was deeply touched to be able to do so. When she was baptized, she teared up again, not with sadness, but with expressions of joy and happiness. My father-in-law, watching the baptism service, also teared up with excitement and joy, saying, "This kind of experience in being a good neighbor to Cubans with spiritual needs is a great blessing and joy." My response: "I fully agree."

The Cubans we met were kind hosts and certainly good neighbors to us, expressing a desire to see government relations between our two countries improve so that there would be more freedom to travel, communicate, and share between our countries. Our leader continued to express his deep love for Cuba and Cubans every time we met at home church assemblies. Cubans were quick to respond in kind. I was also greatly blessed to get to go on three additional mission trips with Rob and Sandy to the Havana area, and one trip with Cletus and Marveena Lynch to Batista in eastern Cuba.

Mission trips like these are helping to improve relations between our two countries. Improved relations can benefit both countries. Cuba has beautiful scenic and historic sites. The warm winter climates and beautiful historical sites there invite tourism from the US and other countries. This could further improve the Cuban economy and provide great travel experiences for tourists. My fervent prayer is that we can lay aside past issues and work together now to be good neighbors. In helping empower each other, we can bless each other and glorify God.

ADDENDUM 2

GOOD NEIGHBOR DEEDS THAT LED ME TO A LOVING RELATIONSHIP WTH GOD

A s neighbors, we often need help from others. To be a good neighbor to the one in need, we must not only see the need but have compassion and give of ourselves to help meet that need in a way that leads to empowerment.

What is the greatest need that each of us has? The Bible succinctly defines it as grace and mercy and a righteous relationship with God and eternal life. Because we are born into sin, we are separated from God, facing eternal judgment and damnation. God created each of us out of His great love for us. He has a plan for each of us to prosper us, not harm us, and for us to have a future and eternal hope and a plan for each of us to be rescued/restored to Him when we seek Him with all our heart (Jer. 29:11-13), To have a righteous relationship with God, there must be atonement for sin. Out of his great love for all mankind, He sent His Son, Jesus, to be that atonement, the "permanent sacrifice," by allowing His Son to be crucified and die on the Cross. Out of His great power, He raised Jesus from the dead and then took Him to heaven to sit at His right hand. God offers this precious gift of salvation, restored relationship, and eternal life to all who repent. "... confess with your mouth, Jesus is Lord and believes in your heart that God raised him from the dead. For it is with your heart that you believe and are justified, and it is with your mouth that you confess and are saved" (Rom. 10:9-10).

I did not fully recognize this greatest need in my life until I was forty-eight years old. I was born to parents struggling with lots of issues. I was exposed to Christianity early in life but was so caught up in conditional love that I tried to earn a relationship with Jesus. I also developed an inferiority complex that I struggled to overcome. My inferiority struggles interfered with my ability to see the unconditional love God wanted me to have.

Here is the background to my early life. I grew up in rural Northwest Florida on a family farm. I was the fifth born of six children. My father and mother married in 1929. He had a great first job working with the Plant Quarantine Board in Central Florida, but within months he was laid off because of the Great Depression and not able to find local employment. They returned to Winston County, Mississippi, where my father started farming in partnership with his father. The Depression created lots of continuing economic hardship for them. In addition, summer drought resulted in poor crop yields and lost profits. My parents had great support from his father and friends but did not succeed at farming in Mississippi. My father was able to work some, helping his father operate a sawmill. My mother became pregnant that December. Then, two bad things happened. First, when my father was cutting down a tree, it fell across another tree. The trunk bounced up, hitting and breaking his chin. Second, on a cold winter night, they built a fire in the fireplace to provide warmth for the baby. My mother woke up sometime after midnight, seeing light and thinking that dawn was coming. She then realized that the house was on fire. The fire spread quickly, and the house completely burned within minutes. They barely got out alive and unhurt with the baby. Their total possessions were one change of clothes and their Model T Ford.

The door to farm life in Mississippi closed abruptly. They returned to Hawthorne, Florida, to stay with my mother's mother. With the New Deal program, there was an effort to establish vocational agriculture programs in high schools. My father checked into this and learned that several vocational agriculture teaching opportunities were becoming available for college graduates with teaching certificates. He already had a master's degree in Agriculture Engineering, so he enrolled again at the University of Florida to get a teaching certificate. He and Mother were living in her mother's boarding house at the time. He received the teaching certificate in the summer of 1931 and learned from the State Vocational Agricultural leader that there was a Vocational Agriculture teacher position in rural northwest Florida at a little place called Jay. He applied for and received the job. My parents again loaded up the Model T Ford and moved to Jay. About the time of the move, my mother discovered she was pregnant again.

My father was obsessed with having a son. He wanted a son very much to keep the Woodruff name alive. He was reminded often that real men fathered male children. In February, after my parents were getting settled into the Jay community, my mother gave birth to a second daughter, my sister Patricia. My father, of course, was disappointed as he was hoping for a son.

Life seemed to be improving for my family. The teaching position was going well, and my father and mother were getting acclimated and accepted within the community. They now had steady and adequate income for the first time, even though the Depression was still in full swing. My father fell in love with the land around Jay. It was flat, red, fertile, and far superior to the lands of central Mississippi. A forty-acre tract of land with a house came up for sale in 1933. My father, without hesitation, bought it and moved his family into the house. At about that time, mother became pregnant again. She was not happy about having another child as she was already caring for two little ones less than three years of age. On September 10, 1935, my mother gave birth to Mary, her third daughter. My father was quite disappointed; his ego and dream of having a son were on the line. Some men in the community began kidding him about his manhood. His frequent response was, "I'm going to have a son, even if it takes filling up the backyard with girls to do so."

Life after that at Jay improved for my family. My father not only taught Vocational Agriculture but also provided education and help to local farmers with agriculture needs. My parents and older sisters became adapted to the community. They made many friends and joined the local Methodist Church, where they attended regularly. In 1940, mother became pregnant for the fourth time. There was much anxiety for her, knowing that my father was desperate to have a son. On September 30, 1940, Mother gave birth to my older brother, H.T. My father was overwhelmed with joy. His dream and desire had come true. With great joy, my brother was named Hiram Toliver Woodruff, Jr. He grew up being called H.T. My parents, at that point, decided that they had enough children, especially with rationing of food and other staples in the early stages of World War II.

Family life was challenged again in 1942. Early that spring, my father took Vocational Agriculture students to the State FFA Convention near Tampa, Florida. While he was away, mother was not feeling well and arranged to have a close friend take her to Century, Florida, to see the family doctor. It was cold that day, so the lady caring for my older siblings fired up the wood stove for cooking and heating the house. She stepped away from the house for a few minutes to gather eggs or something from the garden. As she turned back to the house, she was startled to see the house was on fire near the chimney. She rescued my older siblings and nothing else. The house burned to the ground quickly; no material thing was saved. My mother came home and was distraught to learn about the fire. The next day, my father returned to Jay with the Vocational Agriculture students and learned in town of the family tragedy.

He fussed at Mother a great deal about her being away at the time of the fire and was not happy at all to hear that the doctor thought she was pregnant again. The next six months were difficult for my parents. They were still paying for the land they had purchased and had lost all the appliances that they had bought on credit. Money was tight again and they did not have a place to live. My father had recently built a chicken house. In desperation, he moved the chickens out, cleaned up the chicken house, and moved his family into it.

On September 8, 1942, when my mother went into labor, the family doctor, Dr. Stallworth, came to the chicken house and delivered me into the world. Mother told me that I was sick much of the first year of life, and there were times when the family thought that I might succumb to sickness of one type or another.

It is sad to say that my brother and I were favored in many ways over my sisters. My father expected all his children to labor, helping tend crops and animals and do household chores. All of us had work projects before and after school and full-time farm work during the summer months. Family acceptance was largely shaped by conditional love. For my brother and me, our father assigned us projects where he would share half the income with us, money that was placed into savings accounts for us to pursue a college education. He did not do this for my sisters. My father showed favoritism toward my brother on many occasions. Seeing this gave me a feeling of inferiority. I was always trying hard to please and win my father's favor. Despite all my efforts to impress my father, he almost always showed favoritism toward my brother. My brother never took advantage of the favoritism; he and I grew up as close friends. My early life was more focused on getting than giving of self. It lacked in being the good neighbor to family and others than it should have been.

When I was eight years old, my father said one Sunday morning, "Boys, I think that it is time for you two to profess Christianity and join the church." Without hesitation, we did so, wanting to please him. My father meant well, telling everyone thereafter that the two of us were young Christians. Although I had attended Sunday school and church regularly, I hardly knew what it meant to be a Christian. Honoring my earthly father gave me no conversion experience of accepting and trusting Jesus as Savior and Lord. I grew to adulthood struggling with a sense of self-worth and trying to earn a relationship with Jesus. I participated in church youth activities, later taught Sunday School, and even served on the administrative board of the local Methodist church. But I had no peace and assurance about my relationship with God.

Looking back, it is easy to see how God and friends guided me away from Satan's grip. My failure was trying to be good and do good to earn a righteous relationship with God in the same way that I tried to earn an acceptable relationship with my earthly father. In all my efforts, I found no joy and peace and assurance in truly knowing and trusting God.

My career with The University of Georgia involved providing Extension soybean education programs for Georgia soybean and minor oilseed producers. In addition to preparing educational materials for profitably growing oilseeds, I provided local training programs that allowed me to directly interact with county agents and farmers. Since much of the Georgia soybean acreage was in east Georgia, I spent a lot of time traveling there to conduct field trials and participate in crop training program.

Working in east Georgia required that I spend a lot of nights on the road and away from home. Rural towns then usually did not have good motel accommodations. To my dislike, I found many to be "roach motels." In 1990, the Louisville Motor Lodge was built in Louisville, Georgia. In September 1990, I had a production meeting scheduled in Louisville and was eager to arrange to stay at the Louisville Motor Lodge because it was new. That I did! I checked into the lodge, left my suitcase there, noticed that the room was nice and clean, then left for the meeting with the growers. After the meeting, I returned to the room to prepare for the night. As I got in bed, I noticed a handwritten note on the bedside table. I picked it up, it read:

Dear guest, I have prayed for you today

- That you find accommodations here clean, that they meet your expectations
- That you get a good night's rest
- That you know Jesus as Savior and Lord; and

- And that if you have any doubt about your relationship with Him, that you will take the Gideon Bible here and read Romans 3:23, 6:23, and 10:9-10 (Signed, Betty, motel maid).

The note really got my attention. I had come to the point where I was really wondering about my relationship with God. It seemed that the harder I tried, the less peace I had. In response to the note, I reached into the bedside table and took out the Gideon Bible. I looked up Romans 3:23; it read, "For all have sinned and come short of the glory of God." I knew enough to know that sin separates one from God. At that point, I started coming under conviction and began realizing that all my efforts to earn righteousness were futile. Needless to say, the verse really got my attention for the first time. I then turned a few pages to Romans 6:23, and read, "For the wages of sin is death, but the gift of God is eternal life through Jesus Christ our Lord." Sitting on the side of the bed, I really began to struggle with the verse, first with, "For the wages of sin is death." Yes, I was sinful. Then I pondered over the remainder of the verse, "but the gift of God is eternal life through Jesus Christ." At that moment, I began to realize, eternal life is a most precious gift, not something that can be earned by working hard or doing good, which is what I had been trying to do.

In my sinful nature, I began to argue with God. "God, you know I go to church regularly, I teach Sunday school, I serve on the administrative board, and I support charities." Also, I thought "God, You know I'm not like old Keith. He has cheated on his wife several times; I have not done that. I'm not perfect, God, but You know I work hard to do my job, take care of my family, and serve You." A lot of defensive thoughts continued to come to my mind, but the Holy Spirit revealed to me, "John, you know about Jesus in your head, but you do not have a heart relationship with Him. I then turned to Romans 10:9-10 and read verse 9: "If thou shall confess with thy mouth, the Lord Jesus, and shall believe in thine heart that God raised Him from the dead, thou shalt be saved. For with the heart, man believeth unto righteousness, and with the mouth, confession is made unto salvation." These verses further revealed my problem; especially that I had head knowledge of Jesus but not a heart relationship with Him.

I really began to do some soul searching. Will I receive the wages of sin or the gift of life? Am I trying to justify my faith by good works? Do I just have a head knowledge of Jesus? This would be a beautiful Gideon testimony if I could tell you that, right then, I got on my knees, confessed my sins, asked forgiveness, and started trusting Jesus as Savior and Lord. I did not, but I did come to grips with being lost that night. This did start a soul-searching journey for the next seven weeks. During this time, I began to realize that most of my life had been influenced by conditional love and not the unconditional love of God.

Church friends got me to participate in the South Georgia Walk to Emmaus No. 11 the first week of November. Through that wonderful, loving experience, I came to the time of "Dying Moment," kneeled at the cross in the chapel, and prayed asking Jesus to come into my heart. It was at that point that I truly knew Jesus as Lord and Savior. Going home after that weekend, I overflowed with peace and assurance, knowing that Jesus was my Lord and Savior.

My turning point for trusting Jesus began back in the Louisville Motor Lodge when God used a maid and a Gideon Bible to get my attention and show me that I was missing the mark.

I regret that it took forty-eight years for me to truly come to know Jesus, but I am eternally grateful that God did not give up on me and eternally grateful for the Christian influence of parents, Sunday school teachers, friends, Gideons, and a maid named Betty, who were used by God to point me to Him.

My life story is shared here to identify my greatest need, which is the same as everyone's—that is, the need for salvation, abundant and eternal life. A great need that is fulfilled only by trusting Jesus as Savior and Lord.

May I now wear Betty's hat? In preparing this text, I thank you for reading this book. My fervent prayer for you is that you also address this greatest need if you have not already done so. If you are trying to earn your salvation like I did, you cannot. It is a gift available through the love, grace, and mercy of God. If you have any doubt about your relationship with God, may I ask you, like the maid Betty asked me, to also carefully read and study Romans 3:23, 6:23, and 10:9-10?

If you are really committed to having a Good Samaritan loving relationship with neighbors, you must first have a loving heart relationship with God and be sensitive and obedient to His leading and guiding.

Know this: we are all created by God for an agape love relationship with Him and our neighbors. He does not force us to love Him or our neighbors, but His heart desire is that we love both him and our neighbor. I thank God if you are in relationship with Him through trusting Jesus as Lord and Savior and are sharing His heart's desire with your neighbors. If you are struggling with the command of, "Go and do likewise" for telling neighbors about God's love for them and His plan for them to be in relation with Him, pray and seek His leading. Most churches have great resources for sharing the good news. If needed, check with your church leaders to see what is available. Also, consider starting or joining a prayer and care group to reach out to neighbors with this greatest of needs.

If you have doubts about your relationship with God and the plan He has for your life, Love Your Neighbor Ministries would love to share with you the steps to having peace and the love relationship God desires that you have. For help, go to www.Loveyourneighborinistries.com. We would love to help you with this need.

God bless as you seek His love and share His love with your neighbors.

EPILOGUE

Volumes could be written about additional neighbor needs, including those of seniors, veterans, people who are handicapped, and those who suffer from depression, loneliness, hurt, abuse, and other physical and emotional issues. I have shared with you some neighbor needs close to me, and I recognize that all neighbor needs are equally important to God. It is my prayer that you see each neighbor as a special, unique, loved creation of God, and that you seek God's leading to have a heart of love and compassion for all of your neighbors. Know that our society and the world desperately need good neighbors who seek to love others as self and that in following Jesus's command of, "Going and doing likewise" you can not only help meet an immediate need, but also have a positive, powerful influence for helping many neighbors experience God's love and peace. May God richly bless you as you follow in the footsteps of the Good Samaritan.

Many thanks for all you are doing to be a Good Samaritan Neighbor. I challenge you to reach out to at least one more neighbor, maybe a new neighbor on your street, or any neighbor needing to overcome poverty, hunger, hurt, harm, discrimination, or any of the storms of life. Also, if you are a neighbor in need of a love relationship with God, or have doubts about your relationship with God, please, I pray that you will see the website www.Loveyourneighborministies.com for help in meeting that need.

Your Neighbor in Christ,
John Woodruff

ABOUT THE AUTHOR

John Woodruff, a native Floridian, was raised on a diversified family farm. Educated at Auburn University and Virginia Tech as a crop scientist, he has worked for Virginia Tech and the University of Georgia to improve agriculture. His work has been recognized as significant by peers and professional organizations. A member of First Baptist Church, Tifton, Georgia, he has a heart for Christian missions and for serving his neighbors. Mission trips to various countries have resulted from this passion and expertise. Married to Ina for 54 years, they have three adult children and six grandchildren.

CPSIA information can be obtained
at www.ICGtesting.com
Printed in the USA
BVHW091052030321
601594BV00013B/357